Reading at University

www.thestudyspace.com – the leading study skills website

For a complete listing of all our titles in this area please visit
www.macmillanihe.com/study-skills

Reading at University

How to Improve your Focus
and be More Critical

Jamie Q Roberts and
Caitlin Hamilton

First published 2020 by
RED GLOBE PRESS

Red Globe Press in the UK is an imprint of Macmillan Education Limited,
registered in England, company number 01755588, of 4 Crinan Street,
London, N1 9XW.

Red Globe Press® is a registered trademark in the United States, the United Kingdom,
Europe and other countries.

ISBN 978-1-352-00916-3 paperback

This book is printed on paper suitable for recycling and made from fully managed and
sustained forest sources. Logging, pulping and manufacturing processes are expected to
conform to the environmental regulations of the country of origin.

A catalogue record for this book is available from the British Library.

A catalog record for this book is available from the Library of Congress.

Contents

Chapter 8 Reading in Depth   76

Chapter 9 The Assignment-Production Process: Reading, Planning and Writing   81

Chapter 10 Reading Critically (Part 1): Different Ways of Using Information in Your Writing, Including Critiquing   95

Acknowledgements

Many thanks to all the people who helped to make this book happen, from our colleagues to our families. We are particularly grateful to Helen Caunce who guided this book through its many iterations: you pushed us to make the book as good as it can be. Thanks also to Rosemary Maher who saw the book through its final stages and Fiona Hudson who helped with the figures. And just for something different: we thank all those who rise above petty politics and cast a critical eye over all things, including themselves. It is magnanimity that makes the world a better place.

Introduction

It's not about speed reading...

When we tell students we are working on a book about reading strategies at university, sometimes they say: 'Ahh, good! So can you tell me how to read faster?' This makes us think of those charlatans from late-night television in the 1990s who tried to sell dodgy speed-reading systems by capitalizing on people's belief that all that stands between them and success is their slow reading. Of course, it's understandable that students think that reading faster will help them. In any area of study, there are thousands and thousands of potentially useful articles and books, and it would seem that if you could just get through them, you'd achieve high marks. However, speed is not the answer. Indeed, reading quickly might even hinder your performance.

...It's about being an active, purposeful reader

Your reading will be much more effective and you'll achieve higher marks if you are an *active* or purposeful reader rather than a *passive* reader. An active reader knows why they are reading and they have strategies for meeting their needs; they don't mindlessly plough through words hoping that something magical will happen. Some of the many reasons for reading that will be covered in this book include:

- preparing for class
- identifying the main argument in a source
- working out what topics you should explore in an assignment
- finding and using relevant information within a topic
- broadening your understanding of your field of study
- improving your writing

If you still have speed on your mind, the good news is that once you become an active reader, you'll move faster through your sources. This is not because you'll be reading more words per minute but because you'll know how to identify information that's relevant and not waste time reading material that doesn't help.

Whom this book is for

This book is primarily for students who are about to begin university or who are in their early years of undergraduate studies. However, it will also be invaluable for postgraduates and even academics given its exploration of more advanced skills such as 'synthesis' and concepts such as 'the field'. We've found that even experienced students and academics can employ approaches to reading that are overly time-consuming and sometimes counterproductive. Both of us certainly didn't become effective readers until well into our respective PhD candidatures.

How this book is organized

The first part of this book, 'Before you read' (Chapters 1 to 5), well prepare you for reading at university. We'll begin by discussing some of the dubious assumptions you might hold about academic reading. The idea is that the best way to improve is to recognize what you are doing wrong in the first place. Next, we explore the broad purpose of universities and the nature of academic publishing and how this affects how you should read. This leads to an analysis of marking criteria related to reading. We'll then clarify the various sources of information you'll encounter in your studies, from journal articles and academic books to reports and webpages. Finally, we'll say a few words about where and when you should do your reading.

The second part, 'Reading for your classes and assignments' (Chapters 6 to 15), provides practical advice about how to prepare for class and all the ways you can read to enhance your academic work. We begin with an overview of how to make notes, before offering you strategies for gaining a general sense of what a source is about and reading a source in depth. From there, we focus on how reading features in the assignment-production process and we explore how you can be a critical reader. We'll explain how your reading relates to four key academic skills: comparing, contrasting, evaluating and synthesizing. In the later chapters, we explore how you can use your reading to gain a better understanding of your field or discipline and improve your writing. In the final chapter, we discuss how reading widely for pleasure can also benefit your studies.

How to use this book

You don't need to read this book from beginning to end – in fact, to do so would be a poor reading strategy! Rather, pick the chapters that will be useful for your needs as they arise. If you are just starting out at university, you'll likely not even know about these needs until you've attempted a few assignments and received feedback. The following are some common student needs and the parts of the book that address them.

- If you are not sure about what academics are doing when they are publishing, then read Chapter 2 about the purpose of universities and the nature of academic publishing.
- If you are not sure what your markers are looking for in your assignments with respect to reading, then read Chapter 3, which explores marking criteria.
- If you receive comments that your sources aren't of academic quality, read Chapter 4, which discusses the different types of sources you can use in your assignments.
- If you are struggling to manage your weekly set readings, read Chapter 7, which provides you with some techniques for quickly extracting key information from sources.
- If you are having trouble producing assignments, read Chapter 9, which gives you a step-by-step guide.
- If you are told that you need to take a more critical approach in your work, read Chapters 10, 11 and 12, which explore many of the different things you can do with your sources in your assignments, including the challenging skill of 'synthesis'.
- If you want to extend yourself and start to become an expert in your field, read Chapter 13.
- If you want to improve your writing, then Chapter 14 will explain how you can learn to be a better writer by studying the writing techniques of the authors you read.

At this stage, look over the chapter headings and see whether any one topic grabs your interest. And then keep the other headings in mind as you move through your studies.

And remember: it takes time to become a strong reader

Although you can quickly learn certain academic skills, such as how to construct a convincing introduction, becoming a strong reader takes time: usually years. This is because even if you understand all the strategies you should use, successful reading is ultimately founded on having a good understanding of your area of study (your 'field' or 'discipline') and perhaps even of the world itself. As you are building this understanding, you'll spend – even seemingly waste – a lot of time reading things that either aren't helpful or you don't understand. We've all done this. However, even if it doesn't feel like it at the time, these missteps will help you in the long run. You are always learning, even when you think you are struggling. The point is to keep going.

Terminology

In this book, we talk a lot about academic articles and books. Much of the time, we'll refer to a piece of academic writing as '**a source**'. Sometimes, we'll say '**work**' or '**reading**' or '**text**'. These terms are largely interchangeable.

When we say '**field**', we are referring to a broad area of study, such as 'Civil Engineering' or 'International Relations'. Instead of saying 'field', some people will say '**discipline**'. The two terms mean the same thing. We mostly use 'field' because it's a little more flexible. Within any field or discipline, there are sub-fields or sub-disciplines. For example, 'Organic Chemistry' is a sub-field within Chemistry.

By '**course**', we mean a semester-or term-long class that explores an aspect of a field or discipline. So, in International Relations, you might take a course on the relations between China and Japan. (Some universities have '**semesters**', others have '**terms**'.)

When we say '**subject**', we usually mean the focus of an assignment. We use '**topic**' to refer to an aspect of the subject. Thus, if an assignment has good coverage of a subject, it will have explored several significant topics.

We use the term '**synthesis**' to refer to drawing together the work of others in your own work. Synthesis usually involves comparing, contrasting and evaluating others' work.

A '**set reading**' or '**weekly reading**' is a reading that has been designated by the course coordinator. Usually, there will be one or more of these each week for each of your classes. Their purpose is to prepare you for what will be covered in your classes.

Before You Read

Twelve Dubious Assumptions About Reading at University

Introduction

The first step to becoming a more successful reader is to recognize the dubious assumptions you might hold about how you should be reading at university. These assumptions can come from reading experiences in childhood or at school and are responsible for students not using their time efficiently and for failing to extract relevant information. Even intelligent, hard-working and experienced students (and some academics) don't use their time well or produce the work they are capable of because of these assumptions. The discussions in this chapter are all explored in detail in later chapters.

ACTIVITY 1.1

What assumptions do you hold about how you should read at university?

Before we get going, we'd like you to reflect on the assumptions you may hold about the types of things you'll be reading at university and how you'll go about reading them. Answer the following questions:

1. What types of sources will you encounter at university? What makes them distinct from one another and from things like novels?

2. Are some sources of information more trustworthy than others? How will you determine the trustworthiness of a source?

3. Related to this, is the information in academic publications always right?

4. Given that you'll likely be set many readings each week, how will you manage these readings?
5. How will you read for your assignments?
6. How will you ensure that you remember what you have read?

The assumptions

Assumption 1: You read an academic source as you would a novel

Given that many of us learn to read by reading novels, it's understandable that when we are presented with something that looks a fair bit like a novel, such as an academic article or book, we read it as we would a novel. This is how you read a novel:

1. You open it at the first page and start reading.
2. You read every word, stopping only when you get to the end or when you become so bored you cannot go on.

For many of us in our youth, finishing a novel was a great achievement whereas not finishing was shameful. Perhaps you can even remember a parent asking you whether you've finished a particular novel you were reading and saying something like: 'You must finish what you start' (which is usually good advice!). Altogether, when presented with an academic reading, we assume that every word must be read and that doing so is inherently good.

The facts

Pushing through lengthy academic sources because of the belief that doing so is inherently good or because of the guilty sense that you must finish what you start or even just because you are the determined type will usually yield only small benefits and is often counterproductive. You'll likely recall little of what you've read, and you'll have much less time to explore other sources and write your assignments. You might also end up feeling like you're getting nowhere, despite your efforts, and 'burn out'. As teachers, we've seen such scenarios many times. Our advice is: don't be a 'reading martyr'; don't make yourself suffer needlessly.

The 'T' model: breadth of understanding versus depth of understanding

A point we'll return to again and again is that sometimes you'll need to read to gain an in-depth understanding of a source, but a lot of the time you should be reading multiple sources in a more superficial manner to increase your breadth of understanding of your subject. We call this the 'T' model. The vertical part of the 'T' corresponds with reading one source indepth and the horizontal part with reading multiple sources more superficially.

To avoid being a reading martyr, you need to recognize when reading for depth is necessary and when it isn't. The simple rule is that if an assignment requires you to dedicate hundreds or even thousands of words to analysing a single source, then you should spend a lot of time reading this source. An example is if you are required to critically review an article. However, if an assignment requires you to address a broader problem and you'll be dedicating only 10 or 20 words at most to each source you use, then you shouldn't spend very long reading each source. Box 1.1 outlines when you should be reading for depth and when you should be reading for breadth. We'll provide techniques for reading for breadth and depth in Chapters 7 and 8 respectively.

Box 1.1   Reading for depth of understanding and reading for breadth of understanding

Occasions for reading for depth of understanding

- You read for depth when the focus of an assignment is an article or book. This can be the case with presentations, critical reviews and essays. For example, some essays require the exploration of an important text. Such an essay question might be 'Read Kant's *Perpetual Peace* and assess whether his arguments for achieving world peace are feasible'.
- You often read for depth if you are producing a dissertation. When producing a dissertation, you may wish to educate yourself about a key figure or work. For example, if you are a physicist, you might benefit from an in-depth analysis of the work of Einstein. Or if you are a biologist, you might study Darwin's *On the Origin of Species*.

Occasions for reading for breadth of understanding

- You read for breadth when you are undertaking your weekly set readings. You'll likely not have the time to read every word of your set readings. Read for key information (see Chapter 7) and move on.

- You read for breadth when an assignment requires you to propose a solution to a problem. This occurs with both experiment reports and essays. An experiment report usually contains a literature review that surveys the state of knowledge about a subject. Similarly, essays often involve exploring a range of perspectives. An example of an essay question that encourages reading for breadth is 'Should climate change be tackled through geoengineering?' With such a contentious question, and given limited time and words, it's better to learn what many people think than carefully study the thoughts of one person.
- You read for breadth when you are reading to understand your field of study. As we explain in Chapter 13, a field of study has many dimensions, ranging from its history to current debates. You can learn about these dimensions by reading the introductions of multiple sources. Importantly, once you have a good sense of your field of study, you'll find reading for depth much easier.

So, what's the difference between novels and academic sources?

Novels tell a story and usually employ a *chronological* structure. If even a small section is missed, it can be very hard to work out what's going on. And if you don't get to the end, you never find out what happened. Also, it's culturally frowned upon to read the end if you haven't read all the preceding words.

Academic sources, rather than telling a story, usually provide a solution to a problem and this solution is *branching*. For example, for a journal article, the problem is always stated in the abstract (an 'abstract' is a summary of an article that appears at the start) and introduction, and the remainder of the source systematically lays out the solution to the problem. Figure 1.1 illustrates a basic branching structure for responding to the question of whether voting for the leaders of a country should be compulsory. It should be clear that Section 3 ('Arguments for compulsory voting') would make sense even if you skipped Sections 1 ('A brief history of voting') and 2 ('Arguments against compulsory voting'). Because of the branching nature of a lot of academic work, you don't need to read every word of a source to gain value or find what you are looking for. And there's nothing wrong with going straight to the conclusion to find the solution (if the solution isn't already presented in the abstract or introduction).

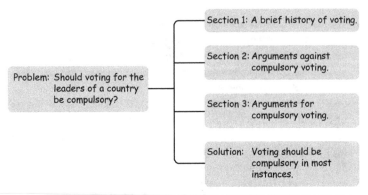

Figure 1.1   **The branching structure of academic work**

Assumption 2: As long as the words pass through my brain, it is good

Closely related to Assumption 1, students sometimes believe that so long as a source is vaguely relevant to a course or assignment and so long as the words pass through their brain, the 'goodness' in the words will remain in their brain for later use.

The facts

Although some people may have amazing memories, the reality for most of us is that words passing through our brains are not automatically stored, especially when these words are not part of a lively story. To gain value from a source, you need to know what you are looking for and have strategies for finding the information. When you find useful information, you should also make a note of it (see Chapter 6). The worst thing you can do is fall into a 'reading trance' where you read and read and take nothing in; this often happens to reading martyrs.

Assumption 3: If I skip something, especially on the reading list, I will miss valuable information

Students sometimes think they must read everything put in front of them since they assume that academic sources are like textbooks and that if they miss a piece of information, their knowledge of their subject will be incomplete and their marks will suffer.

The facts

As we'll discuss in the next chapter, at university the aim is not just to gain knowledge – to learn facts – but to understand a field of study and to be able to solve problems within it. The information that constitutes a field of study can't be collected in a single book: there is too much. Rather, it's dispersed across thousands of sources. Given this, an individual article or book will probably engage with only a small aspect of the field, and, fortunately, different sources will cover similar material. Unless there's an exam to test your knowledge of, say, your set readings, you won't have to read every word of them.

As we'll explain in Chapter 7, when reading both set readings and sources you've found yourself for assignments, you'll be well served if you survey the key sections and get a sense of the types of problems being addressed, the methods used for solving these problems and the respective solutions. It's possible to read 10 to 20 per cent of a source and still understand 80 to 90 per cent of it and find material you can use in your assignments. This is because unlike in textbooks and novels, where important information is dispersed evenly throughout, in academic articles and books important information tends to be concentrated in certain locations: introductions, conclusions and the first sentences of paragraphs. We could say that information in textbooks and novels is 'smooth' but in academic articles and books, it's 'bumpy'. The point is to *focus on the bumps*.

Assumption 4: Academic readings have one meaning and this meaning is correct

In high school, students learn that good marks are achieved by absorbing and reproducing the information in a textbook. Then, at university, they assume that, like textbooks, academic sources have one meaning and this meaning is correct.

The facts

Much of the time at university we read *with* a source; that is, we attempt to learn from a source by understanding the problem being addressed and the proposed solution. And sometimes the source is correct. However, we also read *against* the source. By 'against', we do not mean that we are automatically disagreeing with the source. Rather, we are evaluating the strength of its evidence, comparing the author's position with others' positions, identifying assumptions they might not be conscious of, and so on. A source becomes much richer when you read both with and against it. Furthermore, even when you read with a source, there is immense variety in what you can do with the information. (In Chapter 10, we point out some of the many things you can do with others' work.)

Assumption 5: I do not have the right to have an opinion about what I read

Assumption 5 is closely related to Assumption 4. For many people, the first 20 or so years of life are spent being told what to do and think, to varying degrees, by parents and teachers. This is understandable because parents and teachers have knowledge and life experience and young people need at least some guidance. However, the outcome of this can be that when students arrive at university they lack confidence in their own opinions; indeed, they may not even have well-formed opinions. This can lead to a passive approach to university studies, where they assume that teachers and authors are always right.

The facts

For many, university is the time of transition from being a passive receiver of knowledge to an independent thinker. Even if your opinions are tentative, as is often the case early in your university studies, in most assignments, your marker will still want to hear what you think. Passive regurgitation of others' ideas frequently leads to poor marks (see the marking criteria in Boxes 3.1 and 3.2). A crucial point is that even if you agree with what someone else says, you shouldn't let this person's ideas replace your own; rather, you should explain, in your own words, why you agree or make a similar claim and use the person's work as evidence to support your claim.

Assumption 6: I need to remember what I have read

With novels and movies, it's easy to remember plots or the traits of characters. This is because humans have a special affinity for information packaged in narrative form. It's much harder to remember details in academic sources. This can cause students considerable grief: they feel stupid because what they read doesn't stick in their heads.

The facts

If you need to remember details for an exam, then clearly what you read needs to stick in your head – eventually, however, if you are reading for an assignment or dissertation, it's more important that you make good notes than memorize what you read. Also, memory comes from multiple, and preferably 'deep', exposures to the same information. In the assignment-writing process, going to lectures and looking over set readings provide the early exposures to relevant information. Undertaking assignment-specific reading and making notes constitute further exposures. Deeper exposures occur when you are writing (that is, when you spend time integrating your sources into your assignments and refining your arguments accordingly). And remember, once you complete an assignment, this assignment is effectively an extension of your mind. Keep it and look over it at a later date. Be proud, even if you don't remember every aspect of it!

Assumption 7: First I read, then I write

It's easy to assume that, to produce an assignment, first you read a heap of articles and books and then you write the assignment.

The facts

Although first reading then writing can lead to good assignments, more often, you'll need to move backwards and forwards between reading and writing to produce your best work. For example:

- You'll often do well to begin the assignment-producing process by writing down all that you already know about your subject, based on what you've learned in class and from your weekly readings and from your existing knowledge. In doing this, you'll be establishing topics to discuss in your assignment and starting to think about some of the complexities within each topic. You'll also be establishing terms you can use when searching for sources using your library databases or Google Scholar.
- Later in the assignment-production process, you might find that your writing is stuck. This is often a sign that you need to go back and read some more and fill your mind – and your notes – with topics and arguments you can consider.
- During the editing process, you might find there's a 'gap' in your argument or that you've made a claim without substantiating it with evidence. In such cases, you'll also need to go back to the literature.

We go over all of this in Chapter 9.

Assumption 8: I need to be a fast reader

As teachers, we sometimes hear students speculate that their unsatisfactory marks are a consequence of slow reading. They imagine that the other students – the ones who do well – are flying through a page a minute and stuffing their brains with knowledge.

The facts

You do not need to be a fast reader to succeed at university. Sure, when tested, some students will be able to read 400 words per minute, and others will be closer to 200; however, every reader needs to slow down substantially when they read technical material, which is the bulk of academic writing. In this slower reading environment, it's much more important that you are a *strategic* reader. As we've discussed, you can gain a lot from reading even a small portion of a source – often the introduction and conclusion – if you have a clear purpose and good strategies in place.

Also, reading quickly is not the same as scanning (see Chapter 7). Scanning is a superficial (though not in a bad sense) approach to reading where you are searching for relevant information. When scanning, you keep in mind the information you are looking for (this is your 'filter') and move quickly over the words until you find it. You'll not absorb much of what you read. When you find potentially relevant information, you'll slow down and work out how exactly it can help you.

One thing that does prevent people from reading faster is 'subvocalization'. Subvocalization is when a reader says the words they are reading in their head rather than letting the words pass into their mind. It's easy to work out if you are a subvocalizer. If you are, practice reading without subvocalizing and your reading speed will increase.

Assumption 9: I need to understand everything I read

Students often feel a great deal of pressure to understand everything they read, and they feel stupid when they can't understand an aspect of a source.

The facts

There's a lot to say about this.

- To understand an individual source, often you need to understand the broader field in which it's located. However, it takes time to learn about all the relevant concepts and theories used in your field as well as your field's history, its key debates and the problems it addresses. You'll have some understanding of these by the end of your undergraduate degree. Your understanding will be deeper still if you complete a PhD. But, even then, there is further to travel.

- Unless you are being tested on your understanding of a particular source, you can still score high marks in a course if you focus on a subject and related readings that you do understand. In many courses, you have a choice of assignment questions. Be strategic: play to your interests and strengths. This is what academics do.
- Sometimes, something is difficult to understand because it is an unresolved problem; in other words, no one understands it – or at least no one has the solution! Perhaps there is conflicting or incomplete evidence. Perhaps there are competing arguments that are equally plausible. If you think you are dealing with such a problem, then consider explaining, in your assignment, why the problem is so challenging. Remember: recognizing and exploring the complexities of a problem lead to high marks even if a definitive solution cannot be presented.
- Sometimes, something is difficult to understand because it has not been explained well. The fact is that some academics are better at communicating their ideas than others. Academics themselves frequently discuss the art of writing: some champion plain English (including the authors of this book), whereas others prefer a more 'poetic' approach (for instance, those who follow the tradition of twentieth-century French philosophers).

Assumption 10: All information is created equal

Less experienced students assume that it doesn't matter where they find their information. For example, they think that information found through a Google search has the same credibility as an academic article; or, what's more likely, they don't understand what's special about academic publishing.

The facts

The best academic sources go through a peer-review process. This means that other scholars in the field, along with an editor, read and assess an article or book before it's published, usually making many recommendations about how it can be improved. Most websites and blogs do not employ a rigorous peer-review process, and because of this their credibility is reduced. The peer-review process doesn't guarantee that information is correct; however, it does help ensure that the claims made are consistent with the evidence presented. We'll discuss peer review in Chapters 2 and 4.

You also need to take account of when a source was produced. Sometimes, older sources are 'classics' and contain information to which people still return. Sometimes, they have been entirely discredited and are useful only for understanding the history of a field.

So, what about Wikipedia? Although Wikipedia is an excellent source for gaining a broad understanding of a subject, it should be only a starting point for your research. This is because Wikipedia articles haven't been through the same peer-review process as academic sources. We'll say more about Wikipedia and similar sources in Chapter 4.

Assumption 11: Reading will solve all my problems

A lot of the knowledge about the world is contained in academic articles and books. Because of this, it's easy for students to think that university success is all about reading as many sources as possible and including them in their work.

The facts

Although reading widely is a good thing, you shouldn't forget that there are still a lot of marks to be gained from sticking closely to an assignment question, employing a good structure and demonstrating critical thinking. Sometimes, students who do these things but do not include dozens of sources in their work still achieve higher marks than students who include lots of sources but are unconvincing in other criteria. The point is to strike a balance between your own ideas and those of others. If you include too many sources, you risk losing your authorial voice; if you include too few, your work will lack credibility. We'll return to this point in Chapter 3, when we discuss marking criteria. See also Chapters 10, 11 and 12 on reading critically.

A different, but nonetheless invaluable, point is that going to class and paying attention and getting involved in discussions – listening and talking – can be just as important as reading. By doing this, you'll be immersing yourself in your field of study and developing your own ideas. We'll say more about this in Chapter 9.

Assumption 12: Being aware of my dubious assumptions is enough to escape these assumptions

It's tempting to assume that once you are aware of your dubious assumptions about reading you'll be free of them.

The facts

As with much of life, recognizing a problem is only the first step toward solving it. Success comes from developing good habits. It might take you several assignments, or even a year or two of study, before you are able to effectively implement the skills presented in this book.

Conclusion

In this chapter, we've introduced 12 of the dubious assumptions that students frequently bring with them to university. Underpinning many of the assumptions is a tendency to be overly passive. As we'll discuss in the following chapter, at university you are being trained to be a creator of knowledge and a creator of knowledge is always doing something with others' work. All of this begins with being an active reader. Another key point that we returned to several times is that, in many instances, you really shouldn't be reading every word of every source you come across. There isn't enough time. Unless the assignment requires it, it's usually better to extract the key information from multiple sources rather than study one source in depth.

2

The Purpose of Universities, the Nature of Academic Publishing and What This Means for Your Reading

Introduction

As we've noted, one of the most striking things about studying at university is that there's so much to read. The amount of reading can be daunting, especially if you have just come from studying at high school, where often everything you need to know for a subject is condensed in a textbook. The reading material you are exposed to at university is different because universities have a different function compared with high schools. In short, high schools impart knowledge to students whereas universities both impart and *create* knowledge. Indeed, you yourself are being trained to be a creator of knowledge. In this brief chapter, we'll explain how the function of the university itself relates to the reading material you'll encounter in your studies and how you should engage with it. We'll also outline the standard publishing process so you can get a good sense of what goes on behind the scenes.

ACTIVITY 2.1

What does university mean to you?

Stop and think about what university means to you. Consider these questions:

- Why do universities exist? What is their function in society?
- Why are you going to university? What do you think you'll gain from your university education?
- How will understanding the purpose of universities help you with reading for your assignments?

The purpose of universities and how this relates to reading

As we've begun to discuss, high schools are concerned mostly with knowledge dissemination. That is, students are expected to learn information that is widely agreed by experts to have the status of knowledge. This information is usually contained in textbooks. Generally, the successful student will demonstrate that they have gained the relevant knowledge by reproducing it in an exam or assignment. Universities are also concerned with knowledge dissemination. Furthermore, many subjects have textbooks and use both exams and assignments to assess whether a student has gained the necessary knowledge. Such subjects are found largely in the natural sciences (for example, Physics and Chemistry), applied sciences (for example, Engineering) and formal sciences (for example, Mathematics). However, universities are also concerned with knowledge creation: they are in the business of discovering new things about the world and the universe. Often, this takes the form of solving specific problems (for example, trying to understand the political climate in a country or working out how to improve the strength of a beam without increasing its weight and cost). But it can also be more exploratory. For example, perhaps there is limited knowledge about the biodiversity in a certain region or about what occurs when two substances are combined. Importantly, knowledge is created by building on existing knowledge.

Although students in the early stages of their studies are not expected to create knowledge, they are nonetheless being set on this path and are expected to increasingly demonstrate the skills that are characteristic of knowledge creators.

But how does this relate to reading at university? Two facts are relevant. First, textbooks aside, what is published in articles and books is not knowledge as such but a candidate for becoming knowledge. The point of publishing is to present your claims to the world along with the evidence and reasoning that support them, so they can be scrutinized. Some claims come to be widely accepted and gain the status of knowledge and sometimes are even cemented in textbooks. Others fall by the wayside and become footnotes in the history of a subject. Second, a field of study or even a specific subject is composed of thousands of articles and books, each making their own knowledge claims.

These facts affect how you should read and they do so in three ways:

1. You won't have time to read everything that is relevant. Therefore, you'll need strategies for efficiently extracting key information from sources.
2. A source can rarely be understood in isolation: a source becomes more meaningful when it is read in relation to other sources and the field more generally. Thus, reading at university is usually comparative.
3. Given that what is published is not necessarily knowledge and given that you are being trained to be a creator of knowledge yourself, you should always question – or be critical of – what you read.

Being efficient, being comparative and being critical as a reader are not separate skills: they happen at once. Much of the remainder of this book will explain how to gain these skills.

The journey to a published article

So that you can better understand the knowledge creation process and how this affects the way you read, we'll detail the stages an academic article passes through to be published. Academic articles are the most common way that academics present their research to the world. They are published in journals, of which there are thousands. As you'll see, each stage involves different forms of scrutiny by the researchers them-selves, editors, experts and others. Research is not simply a matter of a clever person discovering something and telling the world about it and the world accepting it.

Stage 1: Developing the article

Here, we'll describe two hypothetical articles: one from the Sciences and one from the Arts and Social Sciences. (If you want to learn more about different ways research is conducted, consult Box 13.2.)

In the Sciences, articles often report the outcome of an experiment. For example, a new type of antibiotic is being developed and the researchers want to test the range of bacteria it's effective against. They devise a method for doing this and spend a year implementing the method and measuring the outcomes. By analysing their data, the researchers find that the antibiotic is indeed effective against a range of bacteria. The article is written up, explaining what they did and found. Throughout this first stage, there was much discussion between the researchers and their assistants about their method and their analyses, and advice and feedback were sought from colleagues about many details of the process.

In the Arts and Social Sciences, research can take other forms. For example, Sociologists can identify patterns in the social world not by using a strict scientific approach but rather by immersing themselves in a subject. For example, a Sociologist is studying the Aboriginal art world in Australia. They do this by reading books about Aboriginal art, seeing what is said by artists, politicians, art dealers, gallery owners, collectors, tourism operators, academics and so on. Having done this, the Sociologist identifies the pattern that some people treat Aboriginal art in the same manner as traditional Western Fine Art (that is, they focus on the genius of the individual creator) whereas others study the art in the Anthropological tradition, in which individual works are explored in the light of the culture in which they were produced. The researcher notes that when Aboriginal art is part of the Fine Art world, the Anthropological approach is believed to devalue the art. In her article, she lays out the details of these patterns, providing many examples. Throughout the process of producing the article, she has discussions with people involved in the Aboriginal art world and colleagues.

Stage 2: Selecting the journal

As an article is being produced, the author or authors are also thinking about which journal to approach to publish their work. This is a difficult decision. In any field, there are many journals. Some have a wide focus and some a narrow focus. For example, in Politics, some journals are interested in politics anywhere in the world whereas others focus on one country. Also, some journals have better reputations than others. This reputation is based partly on people's opinions and partly on metrics such as 'impact factor'. The impact factor of a journal is determined by the number of times articles in the journal are cited in other articles. A researcher might first submit their work to a high-reputation journal, have their work rejected and then end up being accepted by their second choice. Sometimes, an article is rejected several times before being published.

Stage 3: The review process

Every journal has its own process for reviewing articles before they are published. It will involve an editor (who oversees the review process) and usually two or three expert reviewers. Figure 2.1 outlines a typical review process. Sometimes, some of the later stages are repeated until the journal editor is satisfied. In Chapter 4, we say more about the review process.

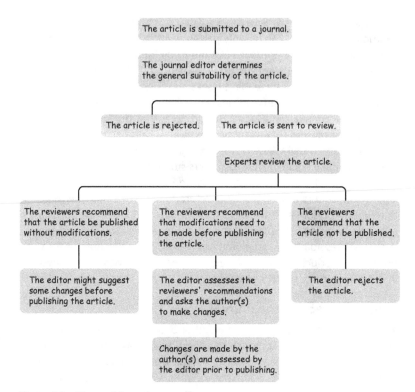

Figure 2.1   The article review process

Stage 4: Dissemination by the broader research community

Once an article is published, it continues to be scrutinized, this time by the broader research community and even by the media and thus the general public, as is the case with more significant research. This is a great thing: it demonstrates that there is a relationship between the creators of knowledge and the rest of humanity, which is as it should be. The following details what happens to articles once they are published:

• Plausible and significant research will be referred to and built upon in more and more articles. It might even make it into textbooks. The discovery of graphene (look it up!) was a recent instance of this.

• Less plausible but still significant research will be challenged by experts. For example, in 2011, scientists announced their finding that neutrinos could travel faster than light. This made headlines because according to Einstein's theory of special relativity, which has been verified experimentally numerous times, nothing travels faster than light. The finding was vigorously challenged by scientists. Within a couple of years, the finding had been demonstrated to be erroneous.

- Plausible but less significant research isn't discussed by other researchers and thus plays little role in the further development of knowledge. Apart from its existence in a journal, it is forgotten. *is promotion important in this?*

Conclusion: so how does understanding the purpose of universities and the publishing process help me read at university?

The simplest response to this question is: you need to see yourself as being part of the broader knowledge-creating community. As such,

- you should draw on published material – arguments, evidence and techniques – in your assignments to solve your own research problems and
- you should, in your assignments, criticize claims that you believe to be implausible.

is there truely such a thing as creating knowledge, or merely categorizing & cataloging existing phenomena? ... humans catching up to nature.

Marking Criteria Related to Reading

Introduction

Having considered how reading relates to the broader purpose of universities, we'll now narrow our focus and explore what marking criteria say about reading. This will give you a practical overview of how your reading should contribute to your assignments. The later chapters will develop many of the points raised here. The marking criteria in this chapter are a combination – or synthesis – of marking criteria drawn from some of the top English-speaking universities from around the world.

The marking criteria

If you survey various marking criteria, both university-wide and discipline-specific, you'll see the same points arising again and again about the relationship between reading and producing successful assignments. Boxes 3.1 and 3.2 provide a summary of these points. Box 3.1 covers what is expected of early-stage undergraduates (first and second year). Box 3.2 is concerned with later-stage undergraduates, especially those who need to produce a dissertation in some form, and postgraduates. In summary the material in the boxes, new students need to build their knowledge and develop their analytical skills. Experienced students need to use this knowledge and these skills to begin to solve significant problems in their field. For each box, we indicate what would constitute a fail, a narrow pass and excellence or high-quality work.

In Box 3.1, we see that to pass, students must largely do what they would have done in high school: demonstrate that they have knowledge

Box 3.1 Assessment criteria related to reading for early undergraduates

	Fail	Pass	Excellence
Reading undertaken	• No evidence of reading/ research	• Reading/ research limited to information provided in class or prescribed texts • Sources found independently are not of academic quality	• Evidence of reading beyond the course content • Sources found independently are of academic quality
Knowledge and understanding	• Gaps in knowledge • Student includes irrelevant or inaccurate information or both • Student demonstrates little understanding of the subject	• Information included is relevant and accurate • Student demonstrates basic understanding of facts and concepts	• Student demonstrates broad understanding of facts and concepts
Use of sources	• Student makes many unsubstantiated generalizations *or* • Student relies heavily on quotations and paraphrases (to the point of plagiarism)	• Some unsubstantiated generalizations *or* • Over-reliance on others' work (work is mainly descriptive)	• Opinions substantiated with well-selected evidence • Information is not just described but analysed • There is some synthesis • Knowledge gained from relevant literature can be applied to different contexts (to solve given problems)

of relevant facts and concepts. Usually, this information will have been provided in lectures and set readings, including textbooks. The stronger students will demonstrate independence by finding other relevant, academic-quality sources that broaden their knowledge.

We also see that weaker students will make claims without providing evidence (a sign of not enough reading) or else their work will largely involve reproducing what others say, by including many overly long quotations or too much paraphrasing (a sign of insufficient independent thinking). In contrast, stronger students will support their claims with evidence and will analyse (break information into parts and assess these parts) and synthesize others' work (combine various pieces of information in a new way; see Chapters 10, 11 and 12). Related to this, they will also be able to generalize from one context to another (that is, apply the patterns identified in one context to another context). (See Box 3.3 for more on this.)

As we see in Box 3.2, while weak assignments at the later stages of study are generally weak for the same reasons as assignments at earlier stages (there is limited reading and poor use of sources), we see a shift in what is required to score high marks. Strong students don't just have analytical skills, they are able to engage with their 'field' or 'discipline'. Even though showing an awareness of your field is necessary only in your later years of study, you'll be well served to start thinking about it from the outset. Chapter 13 is dedicated to this topic. For the moment, it's enough for you to understand that a field is a branch of knowledge or area of study and that every field has its own problems that it addresses, methods for solving problems, history, key figures, debates and so on.

We also see that strong students are increasingly able to master complexity. 'Complexity' is a very important concept. At university, you'll find that most problems you study are complex in nature, meaning that solving them requires you to attend to many, often conflicting, dimensions. This is true if you are building a bridge, and you must balance concerns about materials, costs, the environment, design and so on. It's also true if you are trying to solve social problems, such as what to do about the ageing population, where you must balance concerns about human dignity, economics, immigration and so on.

Finally, we see that strong students demonstrate a high degree of autonomy. They think for themselves about the problems they are addressing and their broader field of study.

Box 3.2 Assessment criteria related to reading for upper-level undergraduates and postgraduates (postgraduate research students are expected to satisfy the 'Excellence' criteria)

	Fail	Pass	Excellence
Reading undertaken	• Student demonstrates little evidence of reading/research • Student is unable to learn independently	• Core readings have been consulted and there is some evidence of additional reading	• Extensive independent reading has been undertaken
Knowledge and understanding	• Student demonstrates limited knowledge or understanding of the field/discipline • Student reproduces knowledge without evidence of understanding	• Student demonstrates some knowledge and understanding of the field/ discipline, including of current problems, and how theories and methods are used to interpret and create knowledge	• Student demonstrates broad understanding of the field/discipline, including a critical awareness of current, typically complex, problems • Student demonstrates mastery of complexities, including contradictory information • Student shows awareness of the limitations of, or ambiguities within, the knowledge base of the field/discipline • Student demonstrates high autonomy in solving complex problems • Student provides new insights
Use of sources	• Student makes unsubstantiated generalizations • Student fails to make appropriate use of evidence • No critical ability is demonstrated	• Some claims or findings are supported by evidence • There are some attempts at synthesis • Critical engagement is limited	• Information is analysed • Student critically evaluates a range of literature in the field/discipline • Sound judgements are made in the absence of complete data

Box 3.3   What does it mean to apply knowledge gained in one context to other contexts?

We saw in Box 3.1 that one characteristic of a strong student is having the ability to apply knowledge gained in one context to other contexts. This might sound challenging, but really it's just a matter of recognizing patterns. The more you immerse yourself in a field of study, the more you'll get a sense of the patterns that characterize it. Sometimes, the patterns will be within the physical world. For example, in engineering, a good student might recognize that if a material functions in a certain way in one context, it may well perform a similar function in another context. At other times, the patterns will be in the social world. For example, in politics, there are always parties that favour a more even distribution of a nation's wealth and others that favour allowing individuals to keep more of the wealth they themselves have obtained. The ability to identify patterns is one of the main attributes of a critical thinker and an expert in a field. When you read, you should always be thinking about how the patterns being discussed in one context can be used to explain a phenomenon or solve a problem in another context.

Conclusion

We saw in the previous chapter that universities don't just provide you with knowledge, they train you to be a knowledge-creator yourself: a problem-solver. We see this philosophy in marking criteria. Weaker and less experienced students can demonstrate they have knowledge, but they can't do anything with this knowledge, whereas stronger and more experienced students can analyse information, explore the complexities of a problem and come up with their own original ideas. Ultimately, these students are on their way to becoming experts in their fields.

The Different Sources Encountered at University

Introduction

As we regularly hear, information has never been easier to access. Almost any book can be obtained cheaply and quickly online, academic articles can be downloaded in seconds for free, and the internet itself is a vast repository of information. However, for students, this is a mixed blessing because it can be challenging to identify which sources are of high quality and which are of poor quality. A Google search on just about any topic will uncover articles and blogs that may look reasonable but whose information might not have been sufficiently scrutinized before being published. Just think about 'fake news': made-up news stories published predominantly on social media to sway public opinion. All of this is relevant to your university studies because when you produce your assignments, much of the time you should obtain your information from authoritative (reputable) sources.

In this chapter, we'll begin by exploring what it means for a source to be authoritative and say a little more about 'peer review'. Next, we'll familiarize you with the typical sources you'll encounter in your studies. We'll also introduce what we call 'non-standard sources'. These include non-peer-reviewed but nonetheless reputable journals, newspapers and magazines as well as 'grey literature', which refers to sources such as reports produced by non-governmental organizations, international bodies (like the United Nations) and corporations. Finally, we'll consider less reputable sources such as tabloid newspapers. The information landscape is changing rapidly, and rather than telling you which sources you must and must not use, we aim to empower you to determine the quality of different sources and how to use them appropriately.

What's special about academic sources?

Before we get into the details of academic sources, we'd like you to think about what you already know about academic sources. Answer the following questions (answers can be found in the chapter itself):

1. What makes a source an 'academic source' and why are students expected to use them in their assignments?

2. How can you tell that a source is an academic source?

3. How do you find academic sources?

4. Should you use non-academic sources in university assignments? If so, how?

Thinking about the authority of sources

So that we can better discuss the different types of sources you'll encounter at university, it's important to understand the two main ways that sources can be used: as 'authority' and as 'objects of study' (the two aren't always exclusive). In this section, we'll explore these two uses and also explain the place of opinion in academic work.

Authoritative sources

When a source is used as 'authority', we are, in essence, trusting that what it claims is true, or in the least, we agree that it is our best approximation of the truth. An important point is that authoritativeness lies on a continuum. The following are four common ways to measure authority in an academic context:

1. Peer-reviewed research that is published in the top journals and by reputable publishers is the most authoritative.

2. Empirical research that has been replicated tends to be more authoritative than research based on argument alone.

3. Research that is published by individuals with strong reputations in their fields is the most authoritative (although individual pieces of research should always be judged on their merits).

4. Research – regardless of where it was published, who produced it or how the claims are substantiated – can become authoritative because of the reputation it gains.

Once again, much of the time at university, you should be drawing your information from the most authoritative sources in your field.

The place of opinions within the university

When you consider what makes a source authoritative, it's important to understand the role of opinion in the university. People often oppose 'fact' and 'opinion'. However, at university, the distinction is rarely black and white, and opinion, when supported by evidence and reasoning, is valued in many fields. Let's consider the distinction between knowledge creation inside and outside the sciences.

In the Sciences, progress is often made not by overturning earlier research (although this does occur) but by building upon it; that is, the earlier research retains its authority and what we could call 'the pool of knowledge' grows. For example, it's highly unlikely that we'll ever dispute that atoms are made up of protons, neutrons and electrons; however, our understanding of these subatomic particles will continue to grow.

In contrast, other fields (for example, Economics, Architecture, Philosophy, Literature, Sociology, Politics and so on) are often characterized by conflicting opinions, and new research doesn't always increase the pool of knowledge in a definitive sense. This doesn't diminish the fields; rather, it's a consequence of the fact that the fields are concerned with enduring, complex problems, usually of a social or cultural nature, that can't be solved by using empirical techniques found in the Natural and Applied Sciences. An example from Economics is the problem of how governments should respond to an economic crisis like the global financial crisis. Although it's possible to be knowledgeable about economic facts, no one really knows how best to respond to a crisis. Thus, academic publications about such things – even the most authoritative ones – will be characterized by conflicting opinions. Given this, in your assignments within such disciplines, sometimes it's possible only to present a range of informed opinions on a topic and determine which you find most convincing. This is usually how an essay proceeds.

And bear in mind that even if a perspective is not demonstrably true, it's still important to support your arguments with and build upon such perspectives. By doing so, you'll be showing that you've consulted the most authoritative sources in your field and you'll also be contributing to the debate. And remember that much of the time in life we are required to make decisions armed only with informed opinions. Recall that in Box 3.2 one of the criteria for excellent work consisted of 'Sound judgements made in the absence of complete data'.

Sources as objects of study

Any source, regardless of how authoritative it is, can be an object of study. By 'object of study', we mean that the source itself can be used as evidence of a phenomenon, or it can be analysed to reveal information that the author did not necessarily intend to be present. For example, if we analyse an opinion presented in a top Economics journal about how to respond to an economic crisis, we might uncover a subtle political agenda. If we analyse a 'fake news' article that has no authority, we might uncover information about the political inclinations of the people who read and share the article. Even memes can be objects of study. They can, for example, tell us very interesting things about popular attitudes about events, trends in society and so on. But memes, like fake news, are not authoritative. This is because anyone can make an internet meme and post it online: there are no checks and balances as to whether the content is accurate.

What you need to take away from this discussion

Inexperienced students do not recognize that there are degrees of authoritativeness. Most seriously, they treat opinions, especially those from non-academic sources such as blogs and online articles, as authoritative. Also, they do not recognize when an opinion should be treated not as authority but as an object of study that should be critically assessed before being included in an assignment.

Standard academic sources

There are three main ways that academics publish their research:

- articles in academic journals
- monographs (entire books written by one or more authors)
- chapters in edited collections (books on a theme with chapters by various authors)

For many types of assignments, you should derive the majority – and, in some cases, all – of your information from these sources. This is because journal articles, academic books and edited collections all go through a peer-review process. As the name suggests, the peer-review process involves peers of the author(s) scrutinizing a piece of work before it's published. Normally, changes are recommended prior to publication. The peer-review process doesn't guarantee that what is published is true, but it does allow us to have greater confidence in the quality of what's published. Also, the reputations of journals (see the next section) are established over many years, and if a journal regularly publishes work that is subsequently discredited, then the top researchers won't want to publish in the journal, and the journal's reputation will decline. For an overview of the review process, see 'The journey to a published article' in Chapter 2. For an insight into the review process of a specific journal, see Box 4.1 for a discussion of how the journal *Nature* manages peer review.

Articles in academic journals

There are around 30,000 English-language peer-reviewed academic journals in the world (as of 2019) and this is growing. Together, they publish about 2.5 million articles per year. However, outside the academic world, we do not often hear about them. The exception is when there is, say, a notable medical or scientific discovery. For example, at the time of writing this chapter, it's been reported in the news that scientists have discovered a new space in the Pyramid of Giza and that their research was published in the journal *Nature*.

Every field has many specialist journals, some of which focus on sub-fields. There are also many journals that are 'interdisciplinary', meaning that they publish material that is relevant to many fields. *Nature*, for example, describes itself as 'the weekly, international, interdisciplinary journal of science'. Also, in any field, there is a hierarchy of journals; that is, there are usually a few that are prestigious and are harder to publish in. Less prestigious journals, of which there are many in a field, are not necessarily less trustworthy; sometimes, they simply haven't been around for long enough to build the strongest reputation, or they may have a narrow or niche focus. In any case, part of becoming familiar with your field is getting to know the journals within it and their relative statuses. Often, rankings are published, although these are also debated.

How do you know whether a journal uses a reputable peer-review process or, indeed, the nature of its peer-review process? Often, you can get a sense of a journal's reputation simply by coming across the name of the journal regularly in your reading. But you can also go to the source itself, the journal's home page, and do your own sleuthing (see Boxes 4.1 and 4.2 to get a sense of what form this sleuthing takes). But be careful: there are a growing number of so-called 'predatory journals'. These journals look like standard peer-reviewed journals, but they don't employ a peer-review process and often exist for dubious and even fraudulent purposes. If you are unsure about a journal, do some Googling: start by typing into the search bar 'is journal X reputable/legitimate?' You'll quickly learn whether a journal is disreputable because there'll be so many people complaining about it!

How do I find articles in academic journals?

There are several places you can find journal articles.

- **University library search engines**. Most, if not all, university libraries have subscriptions to a vast range of academic journals. Although every university will have its own system, you'll be able to search for and download relevant articles on the library's webpage by using something similar to a Google search. Staff at your university will be able to assist you.
- **Google Scholar**. Many articles that can be found through university library searches can also be found through Google Scholar. It's also possible to link Google Scholar to your university library. This is useful because sometimes Google Scholar will not give you full access to an article but will do so if you can show that you are affiliated with a university. It's good to use different search engines (meaning your library's and Google Scholar) when searching for sources because the different engines will sometimes deliver different articles.
- **Google alerts**. If you've had success on Google Scholar with certain search terms, you can set up an alert, whereby you'll be notified when-ever a new article that matches your search terms is published. To learn how to set up such an alert, search for 'Google Scholar create alert'.
- **Reading lists and snowballing**. A simple way to find useful journal articles is to obtain the articles provided by your teachers on reading lists and then see which sources these articles cite (look at their reference lists). You can do the same for articles you've found yourself. This 'snowballing' approach is standard practice in academia.
- **Serendipity**. You can also make use of serendipity. For instance, first determine the top journals in your field or even just journals you like. Then go to the journal's website and look over article titles and see whether you find one that's interesting or useful. Also, although articles are mostly accessed electronically these days, some libraries will have print copies. Find out where they are, wander the bookshelves and flick through journals. We know of academics whose career direction was determined by a chance encounter with a source.

What does the full reference for a journal article look like?

The following reference is formatted using the APA system (the referencing system used by the American Psychological Association; there are many other referencing systems).

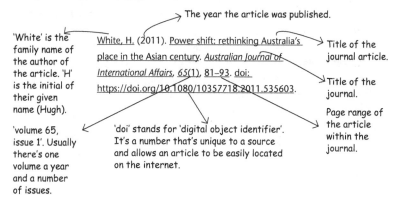

The year the article was published.

'White' is the family name of the author of the article. 'H' is the initial of their given name (Hugh).

White, H. (2011). Power shift: rethinking Australia's place in the Asian century. *Australian Journal of International Affairs, 65*(1), 81–93. doi: https://doi.org/10.1080/10357718.2011.535603.

Title of the journal article.

Title of the journal.

Page range of the article within the journal.

'volume 65, issue 1'. Usually there's one volume a year and a number of issues.

'doi' stands for 'digital object identifier'. It's a number that's unique to a source and allows an article to be easily located on the internet.

Box 4.1   The review process for the journal *Nature*

Nature is a well-known and prestigious journal that publishes a wide variety of scientific articles. On its web page, it provides detailed information about how researchers can publish their research in the journal and the review process. To find this information, we went to the journal home page, clicked 'Guide to Authors' (found at the bottom of the homepage) and then clicked 'Policies' and then 'Peer-review'. (This pathway will likely change; also, we found similar information elsewhere on the site.) What they write about their commitment to advancing knowledge is quite moving. The following are noteworthy points made about their review process:

- Many more submissions are received than can be published. (Recently, the publication rate for this journal has been around 8 per cent.)
- To be published, a paper should 'represent an advance in understanding likely to influence thinking in the field'.
- All submitted papers are first vetted by the editorial staff, not specialist scientists. *Nature* believes that this is best because the editors are not invested in a particular field; they are, in their words, 'unbiased by scientific and national prejudices'. Also, *Nature* argues that whereas specialists have deep knowledge about one field, the editors have a wider context from which to assess the broader worth of a paper.
- Papers that pass the first round of screening by the editors are sent out to two or three reviewers (sometimes more). These reviewers *are*

specialists in the field and thus are well placed to comment on the potential impact of a paper within a field and especially on any technical problems it may have.

- The decision about whether to publish is not about 'counting votes'. Rather, the editors weigh up the assessments of the reviewers, assessing the strength of the reviewers' own arguments.
- There are often follow-up consultations with reviewers to clarify their assessments.
- If the paper is to be published, there are usually two or three rounds of engagement with authors to ensure that all the concerns of the editors and reviewers have been adequately addressed.
- The journal states that their primary responsibilities are 'to our readers and to the scientific community at large'. This is heartening: the journal is committed to presenting the best research, not benefitting individual researchers.

But keep in mind that *Nature* has made mistakes. They've published fraudulent papers and have declined to publish landmark papers or have published them only after appeal, including research that's gone on to win the researchers a Nobel Prize. But importantly, *Nature* readily acknowledges its errors. Furthermore, such errors are an unavoidable part of the process of advancing knowledge. So long as the process is transparent and public, errors can be identified and remedied.

Monographs

A 'monograph' is a book where the entire text was produced by a single author or perhaps two or more authors working together (there aren't chapters produced by different authors overseen by an editor, as is the case with edited collections – see below). This book is an example of a monograph.

As with academic journals, publishers have varying reputations. Although there's no official ranking, it's widely accepted that at the top are the presses of the most prestigious universities, such as Cambridge University Press and Harvard University Press, and also well-established commercial publishers such as Routledge, Sage and Palgrave Macmillan/Red Globe Press.

The peer-review process for a monograph is overseen by the publisher. Typically, an author will present a proposal to the publisher and this will be scrutinized by an editor. (This editor works for the publisher and should not be confused with the editors of an edited collection, who are themselves academics.) If the editor feels the proposal fits with what they publish, they'll send it out for peer review. If the reviewers are sufficiently satisfied with the proposal, a contract will be awarded and the monograph will be written. Once it is written, there will be a further review process involving the editor and external peer reviewers.

How do I find monographs?

You find monographs much in the same way you find journal articles: you use your university library search engine, Google Scholar, course reading lists and reference lists within books and articles. Although many monographs are now published as ebooks, extensive print collections are still common in most libraries. Given this and the fact that books on similar subjects are grouped together, going to a section of the library that is concerned with a subject you are writing about can be an excellent way to find monographs that haven't turned up using online searches. You can even do a tour of other university libraries and see what books they have on their shelves. Often, you don't even have to be a student at the university to look at the book inside the library (though different universities have different policies).

What does the full reference for a monograph look like?

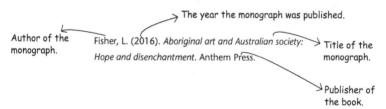

The year the monograph was published.

Author of the monograph.

Fisher, L. (2016). *Aboriginal art and Australian society:*
Hope and disenchantment. Anthem Press.

Title of the monograph.

Publisher of the book.

Chapters in edited collections

It is common for an academic to decide that they'd like to produce a book on a topic and for the book to be composed of chapters or articles written by various authors. Doing this allows a range of experts to contribute to a discussion about a topic all in one place (in a similar vein, journals sometimes have special issues on a theme). Such edited collections will have one or more editors.

Book chapters go through a peer-review process that is similar to the process for journal articles but with a few notable differences. In the first place, the editors will often put out a call for abstracts on a topic (the abstract will provide an overview of the prospective chapter). Having received these, they'll select the ones they think will lead to the most promising chapters. Either before or after this, the editors, having at least one or two sample chapters, will approach academic publishers and present their proposal for the book to secure a book contract. The publishers will scrutinize the proposal and the sample chapters and decide whether to offer a contract. Once the contract has been secured, the writing of the book will be completed. The editors themselves will oversee the peer-review process. Perhaps the authors of the book will review one another's chapters, or perhaps there'll be external reviewers.

Where do I find chapters in edited collections?

You find chapters in edited collections just as you would find journal articles and books.

What does the full reference for a chapter in an edited collection look like?

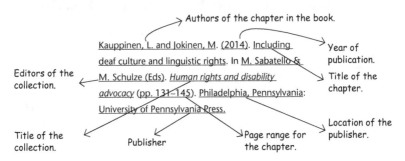

Authors of the chapter in the book.

Kauppinen, L. and Jokinen, M. (2014). Including deaf culture and linguistic rights. In M. Sabatello & M. Schulze (Eds). *Human rights and disability advocacy* (pp. 131–145). Philadelphia, Pennsylvania: University of Pennsylvania Press.

Editors of the collection.

Title of the collection.

Publisher

Page range for the chapter.

Year of publication.

Title of the chapter.

Location of the publisher.

Non-peer-reviewed sources and 'grey literature'

Although for many of your assignments you should be reading and including information from peer-reviewed academic journals, monographs and chapters from edited collections, there will be other useful sources you can draw from, albeit with some caution. These will include non-peer-reviewed publications such as newspapers and magazines and 'grey literature'. 'Grey literature' refers to sources that are potentially authoritative but that haven't been through a peer-review process and aren't published through normal academic channels. Also, often such sources can't be found through university library searches. Grey literature is produced by government agencies, non-government organizations, international bodies, corporations, research centres and so on. We are not able to tell you which sources are the most reputable since there are too many source types and too many bodies producing grey literature. Much of the time, the issue is not whether you should use a source but ensuring that you use a source appropriately. We'll expand on this in the following section.

Establishing the credibility of and using non-standard sources

If you intend to treat a non-standard source as authoritative, as you would an article from a reputable journal, then you need to establish the *credibility* of the source. Consider the following:

- What processes have been used to ensure the accuracy of the information within the source by the publisher?
- Does the publisher have a good reputation?
- Does the publisher have any notable affiliations (these could be political or religious, for example)? Have these affiliations affected the information presented? If yes, does this influence the authority of the source?
- Has the author or publisher received any notable funding for the research? Might this have affected the information presented?
- Is the source well written? Grammatical and typographical errors can be a sign that a source hasn't been sufficiently reviewed.
- Do academics in the field treat the source as authoritative? If they do, then so can you.

If you do determine that a source isn't necessarily authoritative, but rather the bearer of specific values, be they those of a corporation, political organization or something else, you can still use the source, but you should treat it as an 'object of study'. For example, a report that was produced by a non-government organization with funding from a government and that presents the same government in a good light can be extremely interesting to analyse: it can reveal how the government is attempting to market itself to the world, for example.

Other sources can be used as evidence of a phenomenon. These are often referred to as 'primary sources' (once again, we are talking about using sources as 'objects of study'). For example, if a certain meme goes viral, then it's arguably the bearer of a zeitgeist and as such can be worthy of analysis. Perhaps a viral meme reveals more about attitudes at a certain time than a well-crafted survey does. But be careful; every discipline has its own techniques for dealing with primary sources, whether they are memes, a diary or blog entry, or data gathered in an empirical study. If you include information uncritically, your mark will suffer.

Non-standard sources can be a useful source of information, such as facts and quotations, even if you don't trust – or use – their analysis. This is the case with reputable newspapers and magazines. Sometimes, these sources are the only place you can find things like comments by a politician or economist. Even unaffiliated websites can provide useful information. For example, the website technovelgy.com provides a long list of inventions that were first thought of in science fiction. This is a great resource for people interested in the topic. Also, such information can be easily verified.

Finally, some sources can be used as inspiration for analysis or an argument. This is the case with movies, books and other art forms. For example, if you are writing a philosophy essay about the question of whether human rights could be extended to artificial intelligence, you may well mention *Blade Runner 2049, Ex Machina* or *Her*, all of which include prominent non-human characters. None of the movies is what we would call 'authoritative', but they provide interesting perspectives that could be developed. For instance, *Blade Runner 2049* raises the question, 'Is it necessary to be born to be human?' And both *Ex Machina* and *Her* raise the question, 'If an artificial intelligence seems human to other humans, is this sufficient to be considered human?'

In Boxes 4.2, 4.3 and 4.4, we scrutinize several non-standard sources.

How do I find non-standard sources?

Much of the time, you find non-standard sources on the internet; this is the case with most magazines and newspapers and especially government publications, reports by international organizations and so on. But, in some instances, access might be restricted; this could be the case with corporate documents. Sometimes, when you take a course, your teachers will provide a list of websites where you can obtain sources such as annual reports or reports by international organizations.

Are there sources I should never use?

Let us be clear: even though any source can be useful so long as it's used appropriately, the reality for most markers, especially of undergraduate work, is that they encounter too many assignments that draw heavily and uncritically on sources that are found through a Google search. These include Wikipedia articles, blogs and what we call 'random articles'; a 'random article' is a lightly researched, sometimes plagiarized article that is typically produced to attract people to a website so that the website can make money from advertising. These sources can help you become more familiar with your subject, but they are also far more likely than a peer-reviewed source to be erroneous or fail to cover significant points. These sources should not appear in your assignments unless you have a very good reason for including them. The utility of these sources, even as objects of study, will likely be limited. If you do come across interesting facts, theories, or authors through a Google search, you should pursue these by consulting academic sources. We'll say more about this when we explore the assignment research process in Chapter 9.

Box 4.2   Evaluating the authoritativeness of non-peer-reviewed and grey literature: a non-peer-reviewed journal

The Bulletin of Atomic Scientists lies somewhere between a magazine and an academic journal. It can be described as a non-technical academic journal: it discusses significant issues in a non-technical way. Its focus is major threats to civilization, including nuclear weapons, climate change and what it calls 'emerging technologies' (for example, artificial intelligence).

Unlike many peer-reviewed academic journals, whose goal is to publish significant research in a field or sub-field without a specific agenda (other than building knowledge within the field), The Bulletin aims to 'influenc[e] public policy to protect our planet and all its inhabitants'. This is significant because straight away this affects the way you would use the information in it. Specifically, you wouldn't treat arguments made by its authors as unquestionably authoritative but as perspectives on an issue. However, there is certainly nothing wrong with this: as we've mentioned, within the Humanities and Social Sciences and also in debates about how discoveries in the Natural and Applied Sciences should be used, often all we have are educated perspectives.

The magazine admits that it isn't peer-reviewed (this admission adds credibility, as it's a sign of honesty). Yet this is not to say that The Bulletin doesn't exercise conscientious editorial oversight. Furthermore, The Bulletin requires that its authors cite their sources of information. On the 'Write for The Bulletin' page of the magazine's website, we read, 'The Bulletin is not a peer-reviewed journal; however, we do send unsolicited articles to colleagues for outside review. Be prepared to answer questions and to document your points – by way of hyperlinks for web pieces or in the form of footnotes for journal pieces.' The Bulletin also states, 'The articles are edited and, at times, thoroughly re-worked by experienced Bulletin editors. This is worth repeating: Because it is dedicated to excellence, the Bulletin never publishes unedited articles.' Such comments also increase the credibility of the publication.

Finally, despite being non-peer-reviewed, *The Bulletin* still ranks in the top third of International Relations journals.

Should you use *The Bulletin of Atomic Scientists* in your assignments? The *Bulletin* is a good-quality, non-technical journal with a political agenda (or at least a political concern: major threats to humanity). It's great to use if you are exploring different opinions about a contentious issue (for example, if you are writing an essay about the rise of artificial intelligence). However, you should be wary of treating articles as authoritative: all claims within it should themselves be objects of study that you critically assess. Also, as is the case with all non-peer-reviewed sources, it's a good idea to check the credentials of an article's author.

Box 4.3   Evaluating the authoritativeness of non-peer-reviewed and grey literature: reputable newspaper articles, tabloid journalism and fake news

The question of whether you should use newspaper articles in your university assignments cannot be definitively answered. Again, the issue is whether you intend to use an article as authority or as an object of study. All newspapers lean in a political direction. And although this doesn't mean that newspapers in general are untrustworthy, it does mean you must be cautious with how you use their articles.

It's also important to be aware that some newspapers are much more reputable than others: some have their own strict codes of ethics. They publicize, amongst other things, when they make errors, and they fire journalists who plagiarize, lie or exaggerate. Like academic journals, newspapers build their reputations over many years. As a consumer of news, you should always explore the reputations of your news sources. Also, newspapers often publish opinion pieces, which are not limited to reporting the facts but include opinion.

If you want to treat a newspaper article as authoritative, do your best to corroborate the claims in it with peer-reviewed sources. That said, perhaps no corroboration will be required if you are reproducing basic facts, such as statistics or quotations. This is a question of personal judgement.

However, you'll have much more freedom if you want to use newspaper articles as objects of study. Imagine you are writing an economics essay about interest rates. It might be useful to survey what many different economists said about a particular interest rate event, not because they were right but to reveal the range of opinions.

Finally, you should be aware of the phrase 'tabloid journalism'. 'Tabloid journalism' refers to news sources that make their money by exploiting people's fears and desires. They are less concerned with accuracy. They will focus on telling sensational crime stories and will also dedicate many pages to celebrity gossip. Such news sources will claim that they follow a code of ethics, but their practices rarely survive serious scrutiny. Often, tabloid journalism is factually correct; the issue, rather, is how the facts are interpreted. For example, a common ploy is to report an attractive lie by finding a dubious expert who has expressed the lie. At the time of writing, there was a story in Sydney's *Daily Telegraph* (affectionately known as the 'Terrorgraph') about bike sharing. There have been some reasonable discussions about the clutter caused by these bikes. The *Telegraph*, however, published an article arguing that the bikes could be used by terrorists to make bike bombs, citing the opinion of a dubious expert. Strictly speaking, this article is not factually incorrect. But the angle is ludicrous: surely a terrorist could just put a bomb in a backpack or buy their own bike. The point is you should *never* use tabloid journalism articles in an assignment as authority; however, you could certainly use them as objects of study (for instance, as evidence of different public discourses on a topic, such as cycling or terrorism).

And so what about 'fake news'? Fake news is a step below tabloid journalism. Whereas tabloid journalism is about 'spinning' facts, fake news is about lying. The simple point is that given how easy it is these days to create and distribute digital material, people now create fake news articles. Don't trust news articles that appear on Facebook and other social media. Get your news from reputable news sources.

Box 4.4   Evaluating the authoritativeness of non-peer-reviewed and grey literature: a report from a non-government organization

Let's consider the report (or 'Issues Paper') *The other side of gender inequality: men and masculinities in Afghanistan* (the report can be found online). The report was produced in 2016 by the Afghanistan Research and Evaluation Unit (AREU) and the Swedish Committee for Afghanistan (SCA).

First, we should consider why we would want to use such a report. It would be useful if we were writing about some of the challenges faced by Afghanistan; the relationship between Afghanistan and the rest of the world; or gender issues, both within Afghanistan or more broadly. Before using the report, you'd learn what you could about the two authoring organizations. Specifically, you'd find what the organizations said about themselves and also what others said about them, paying close attention to negative comments. We quickly learned that the AREU is an independent research unit and that the SCA is a politically and religiously unbound non-governmental organization. Notably, the SCA plays a substantial role in improving the lives of Afghans through health and education. However, both organizations have an agenda: they are both committed to Western ideals about human rights and democracy. We are not, at this point, saying this is bad – merely noting it. With respect to funding, the SCA is funded by the Swedish government and the Ministry of Public Health in Afghanistan.

What is the significance of all this? There are two notable aspects to the report. The first is the data it provides about attitudes to the roles and actions of men and women in Afghanistan. These data reveal pervasive conservative values (conservative from a progressive Western perspective), namely the belief that the role of a man is to be a provider and protector of the family and the role of a woman is to manage the home. We also read that both men and women accept violence against women in some situations. Such findings are not surprising and could be incorporated in an assignment with high confidence that they are authoritative. The second notable aspect is the recommendations; this is where using the information in the report becomes more challenging. The recommendations all focus on changing Afghan society (albeit by working with various local organizations). These recommendations are debatable and thus it would be reckless to represent them as authoritative. Once again, it would be much better to treat the recommendations themselves as an object of study and discuss them as one perspective amongst others in the broader context of Western involvement in Afghanistan.

ACTIVITY 4.2

Evaluating the authoritativeness of non-peer-reviewed and grey literature

Below are some sources you might consider using in your university assignments. Determine how authoritative they are – or in what ways they are authoritative. Consider if you should you use these sources in a university assignment and, if so, how?

- *The Victorian Web* (http://www.victorianweb.org). This is a website containing many articles about literature, history and culture during the reign of Queen Victoria of Great Britain.
- *The United Nations Convention on the Rights of the Child*
- *Time Magazine*

Conclusion

One of the many challenges at university is finding sources and assessing their quality. There is no simple metric that you can use to guarantee that the information you include in your assignments is true. However, being aware of the different forms that academic publishing takes and understanding the value of the peer-review process are good places to start. The longer you spend in your field, the more you'll become familiar with the sources that are appropriate and with how best to use sources. And remember that sources can be used as authority (you trust what they say) and as objects of study (as something to be analysed to reveal useful information).

5

Optimizing the Environment in Which You Read

Introduction

Before we get into the specific strategies for making your reading as effective as it can be, we want you to think about where and when you read and consider some other details, such as whether you should read printed material or on the screen.

What works for you?

It is said that the words 'know thyself' were inscribed in the forecourt of the temple of Apollo at Delphi in Greece. It is the best advice. To read – and, more generally, work – effectively, you should know where and when you are at your best. Consider the following questions:

- Where have you done your most successful reading and studying? Do you like a quiet, private, indoor space or somewhere busy and outdoors?
- How long have you been able to work before you start to lose concentration? Has this varied with different types of reading?
- What times of the day are you most focused?

Where and when to read

Different kinds of reading can take place in different environments and occupy different amounts of time. This is good news: it means that although you will sometimes benefit greatly from reading in a dedicated work space, other reading can be done in the in-between times, such as when you are travelling or waiting for friends or for a shift to start. The following is an overview of the different types of reading you'll encounter and some suggestions of where and when you can do it.

- Usually, the deeper reading you do for your assignments should take place in a comfortable environment when you have a good block of time – say an hour or two. As we'll explain, this deeper reading will involve finding and evaluating key information, comparing different sources, making notes and planning. This is hard to do in the in-between times as you'll need time, few distractions and space for books, papers, a computer and so on.
- However, if you are reading broadly to prepare for an assignment, this can take place in the in-between times. This is because such preparation often involves skimming through articles, having a look at abstracts on Google Scholar and so on.
- You can also complete your weekly readings in the in-between times and places. As we'll explain in Chapter 7, for these readings it's often enough to extract the key information; this can be done in 10 or 15 minutes, and you might not even need to make notes.

You should block out times each week in which you will do deeper reading; also, be prepared to make use of the in-between times for more general or superficial reading.

Your ideal reading environment

A dedicated workspace is a good idea. This space will function best for you if the following are present:

- A decent-sized desk. You should have enough space to have a computer, a bunch of books and papers all in operation at once.
- A comfortable chair. Some people can sit on anything. Others need something special. Work out what type of sitter you are.
- Good lighting and aspect. A room with a view is an excellent idea. Natural light, trees and water (if you can afford it) are great for morale. Perhaps a desk lamp and potted plant are a viable compromise.
- Good ventilation. Depending on the season and your environment, fresh air can be a plus. But at least have moving air, whether this be a draft or air-conditioning.
- Peace and quiet. If you have a study, that's great. But if you are sharing a room or have a busy home, you might consider using noise-cancelling headphones.

- Favourite objects and sounds. Your workspace will be all the more pleasant if you put things in it that make you happy. This could be pictures of loved ones, an aromatic candle or an amusing Bobblehead figure. You might also like to play music, although for some this might be a distraction. Classical music may work for you, as it doesn't have words.

However, you might also function well in other environments (such as within the energy of a café or common room).The point is: find out what works best *for you*.

Managing reading sessions and working out when you are at your best

Effective reading takes concentration, and you don't want social media notifications interrupting a session of deep reading. You can download apps or software that can help you manage your phone use if self-discipline proves tricky. There are also certain strategies that you might consider using, like the Pomodoro technique, where you read for 25-minute intervals and take 5-minute breaks between sessions.

You should also figure out when your brain is at its best: first thing in the morning, late morning, afternoon or evening. Try working at these different times and monitor your performance. Many people find they are at their best not long after they wake up.

Reading and technology: to screen or not to screen

The increase in the availability of cost-effective technology means that you no longer need to spend hours in the library leafing through dusty back copies of journals, nor do you need to invest in expensive (and heavy) textbooks. Screen readers, tablets, laptops and, increasingly, phones give you access to the vast majority of material that you'll need to successfully complete your courses, including course and assessment content, emails, journal articles and ebooks.

Reading on screen has a number of benefits:

- The ebook versions of textbooks are often quite a bit cheaper than their hard-copy counterparts.
- Digital texts are easily searchable, meaning that you can find specific references to things even if they aren't included in the index.

- You can highlight and leave comments on PDFs, meaning that all your notes are in the one place instead of scattered around different notebooks, memory sticks or cloud platforms.
- You use less paper (although we acknowledge that electronics also have an environmental footprint).
- Digital texts are portable – much more so than traditional textbooks – and you can access them from a variety of devices.

Despite the impressive list of benefits to reading texts digitally, some people prefer to read a hard copy or to read at least some things in hard copy. One of the key advantages to paper copies is that there is no need to worry about batteries running out or patchy internet access, but beyond that, there is a certain pull that many people feel towards paper over screen that they can't entirely explain. Recent research suggests that even 'digital native' children prefer reading books in hard copy rather than on a device (Merga and Roni, 2017), so it's perhaps just one of those funny human quirks.

You might find that you like reading on screen for some activities and reading on paper for others. For example, it may be easier to do an initial literature review on screen, where you can scan through dozens of articles and quickly decide whether or not an article is relevant to your research (see Chapter 7). You may choose to print out a handful of the most relevant articles or book chapters and work your way through them closely with a highlighter and a pencil to make notes in the margin. You might also consider printing out copies of your assignments for your final edit – typos, odd gaps and fonts that don't match can often be easier to see on paper than on screen.

Maintaining concentration while reading

Concentration is tricky. The reality is that academic reading can often be boring. In addition to finding the best places and times to read, there are some other things you can do:

- Most generally, study something that you enjoy or that you see yourself spending a significant portion of your life doing. This might sound trite, but it makes a huge difference. Just think about some of the things you like exploring on the internet – perhaps you follow a sport or have a hobby. The fact that you enjoy it allows you to spend hours and hours reading about it.

- Being an active reader will make whatever you read more interesting. Think of yourself as a player in the knowledge game, not a passive receiver of others' ideas.
- Don't try to read for much more than 2-hour blocks (perhaps you do 4 blocks of 25 minutes with a 5-minute break between each).
- Take long breaks (several hours) between successful blocks. This will give your brain time to process what you've done.

Conclusion

We strongly recommend that, as early as possible, you get a sense of how you read and work best. Which environments do you prefer? What time of day are you most focused? When do you like reading on screen and when might you need to find a printer? There are no right answers to these questions apart from the ones that suit you best. Working out your preferences now will make the reading strategies that we talk about in the rest of the book all the more powerful when you put them into practice.

Reading for Your Classes and Assignments

CHAPTER

6

Making Notes When You Read

Introduction

We begin this part of the book with note-making because all the different ways of reading we'll explore can (and often should) be accompanied by note-making. However, given that the main purpose of this book is to help you produce better assignments, this chapter, especially in the later stages, will focus on making notes for your assignments. (You might like to read it in conjunction with Chapter 9, which details the assignment-producing process.)

The most important point about making notes is that you shouldn't be a passive note-maker. That is, you shouldn't just mindlessly reproduce information; you should record *how the information you read is useful for you*. The following are key questions you should respond to in your notes (the first encompasses all the others):

- **Relevance:** How is the source relevant for my purposes?
- **Topics:** Does the source introduce me to useful topics to consider?
- **Evidence:** Does the source mention useful facts, techniques, arguments, opinions, concepts, theories or figures?
- **Comparing and contrasting:** How is the source similar to and different from other relevant sources?
- **Evaluating:** Do I agree or disagree with the information presented?
- **Synthesizing:** How can I combine the information in the source with the material in other sources?
- **Organizing:** For my assignments, how can I best organize a discussion of the relevant information?

We'll begin this chapter by discussing how *not* to make notes: we'll introduce what we call the 'tragic characters' of the note-making world and explain why their approaches don't help them. Then we'll explore the benefits of good notes and provide you with several note-making techniques for different contexts.

Finally, bear in mind that notes are very much a personal thing and also that the approaches you'll use will vary over time and from one task to another. You might even fix on a technique that isn't as efficient as it might be but that you are comfortable with and that leads to high marks. This is fine.

ACTIVITY 6.1

How do you make notes? How should you make notes?

Before you hear what we have to say about notes, reflect on how you make notes. Answer the following questions:

- How do you make notes?
- Has your approach been useful?
- Were there any problems with your approach?
- Can you think of a better way to make notes?

The tragic characters of the bad-note-making world

In Chapter 1, we introduced you to the 'reading martyr', the student who reads and reads because of the dubious assumption that doing so is inherently good. The reading martyr ends up wasting a lot of time and can receive marks that, they believe, do not reflect the effort they put in. Note-making has its own cast of tragic characters: people who employ questionable note-making techniques and who find that, when it comes time to write their assignments, they have little to say. The questionable techniques are often underpinned by the same flaw from which the reading martyr suffers: passivity. We include this section with the hope that if you yourself are one of these 'tragic characters', then you'll recognize your problems and use some of the strategies in this chapter to fix them.

No Notes

'No Notes' reads a lot but records nothing. The obvious problem with this is that No Notes will have no record of the useful information they came across nor the thoughts they had when reading. When they are reading for their assignments, they do nothing to build a bridge between their reading and writing.

The Copying Martyr

'The Copying Martyr' has a very different problem from No Notes: rather than writing nothing, they copy out everything they read. However, even though they feel like they are being active, they are ultimately being passive because they are not being selective nor thinking about how the information is useful for their purposes. It's probably worse being The Copying Martyr than No Notes because The Copying Martyr wastes so much time, especially when they make copious notes about their weekly readings (which require very few notes).

The Highlighter

'The Highlighter' is a relative of No Notes. While reading, The Highlighter highlights important passages, but they don't make a note of why the highlighted passages are useful. When they look over what they've read, they ask themselves, 'Why did I highlight that?' And because they don't remember, they have to reread large sections of the source to remember. Highlighting is only a little better than making no notes at all.

The Summarizer

'The Summarizer' will read an entire article and summarize it. Although summarizing might seem valuable, it has two problems. First, the Summarizer is still being overly passive because they are not thinking about how the material is useful for them (which is essential if you are producing an assignment). Second, carefully reading and then summarizing an entire article is often a waste of time. Keep in mind that abstracts, some introductions and conclusions are themselves summaries, and so if all you want is a summary, you don't really need to read much more than these sections.

The Abstract Expressionist

Like Jackson Pollock (look him up), 'The Abstract Expressionist' throws all sorts of ideas into their notes, but they do so in an indiscriminate manner, such that when they look at their notes later they can't make any sense of them. Quotations, summaries, paraphrases, ideas, structural diagrams and other elements are all jumbled together. So, although The Abstract Expressionist is at least starting to develop their own ideas in their notes, the bridge they are building between their reading and writing will likely fall down when they put any weight on it – when they try to produce their assignment from their notes.

The Bad Housekeeper

Our final character, 'The Bad Housekeeper', records useful information and their ideas about it, but they leave out important facts such as bibliographical information (for example, authors and titles) and page numbers, so that when it comes time to reference the material in their assignments, they are unable to do so because they don't know where they found it. They then have to comb through their readings to re-find the information, which takes time and is, more often than not, a soul-destroying process full of self-recrimination.

What do good notes help you achieve?

Having met some of the tragic characters of the bad-note-making world, you should have a clear idea of what good notes help you achieve.

Good notes assist memory

Notes assist memory in two ways: they function as an external memory and they help you lay down memories. In more detail: First, whether you are preparing for class, working on your assignments, pondering the nature of your field or discipline or admiring the prose of a good writer, you'll not remember everything you read, so you need to have a record of the information you thought was useful when you read it and perhaps also the thoughts you had about it. Second: to gain expertise in your area of study, naturally you need to learn a lot about it. However, the way the human brain works, it's often not enough to be exposed a relevant idea once: what is needed is repeated exposures and deep processing. So, reading something gives you one exposure, but then copying out a quotation gives you a second exposure. If you explain how the information will be useful for you, you will have introduced deep processing. And if you go on to use the material in an assignment, you will experience further exposures and undertake further deep processing.

Good notes help you develop your ideas

If you are to be an expert in your field of study – which is the ideal outcome of a university degree – then you'll need to have your own ideas about many aspects of your field. A great place to develop these ideas is in your notes; this is regardless of whether you are undertaking your weekly readings, working on an assignment or reading independently because of curiosity. Your ideas will range from identifying patterns, making critiques, thinking about how different perspectives or techniques can be applied or combined, and so on.

For your assignments, good notes make a bridge from your reading to your writing

When working on your assignments, by taking note of the topics you might discuss, the complexities within topics, contrasting opinions, your opinions and so on, you'll be assembling the *components* that will go into your assignments. The idea is that once you have assembled the components, you'll then put them together. Students struggle to write when they don't make notes since they don't have the components they need.

Good notes help you get more marks in less time

Even though notes take time to produce, they ultimately save you time because you won't need to go back and reread sources to find the relevant information and remember your best thoughts. And because your ideas are better developed when it comes time to write, you'll find it easier to write and your written work will be stronger.

Good notes help you avoid plagiarism

If your notes are disorganized – if you are an Abstract Expressionist or a Bad Housekeeper – you'll be in danger of committing plagiarism. This is because if your notes are not well organized, you might draw ideas and quotations from them and not even realize they were produced by someone else. Good notes can help you avoid plagiarism in another respect: plagiarism sometimes occurs when students don't have any of their own ideas because they didn't go through the process of developing them. They then fill their assignments with quotations or a stream of connected paraphrases such that their own voice is absent.

Note-making in different contexts

As mentioned, this book, for the most part, is concerned with helping you produce better assignments, and most of our discussions of note-making in the remainder of this chapter contribute to this end. However, you can make notes in several additional contexts (details can be found in the respective chapters). You can make notes about the following:

- your set or weekly readings (see Chapter 7)
- foundational and often challenging texts (see Chapter 8)
- your field (see Chapter 13)
- how to write (see Chapter 14)
- wisdom you've encountered in your wider reading (see Chapter 15)

Making notes for your assignments

You should read this section in conjunction with Chapter 9: The Assignment Research Process. When making notes for your assignments, there are two main questions:

1. How many notes should you make?
2. What should your notes look like?

How many notes should you make?

It's extremely important that the amount of notes you take about a source, and indeed the amount of time you spend reading it, *are proportional to the amount you will write about it*. In short: if you aren't going to write much about a source, then don't write a lot of notes about it. There are, roughly speaking, three levels of importance for sources.

1. **An entire assignment is focused on one or perhaps two sources.** This is the case with critical reviews (which involve summarizing and evaluating a source) and some essays (which can involve exploring a key article or theory, creative work and so on). If you are going to write over 1,000 words about a source, then it makes sense to spend at least several hours reading and rereading it and making notes about it. Your notes could include an overview of the source (you'll likely need such a summary anyway in your assignment), key points, your own critiques and others' critiques (if you are writing about an important article or theory, others will have published about it).

2. **A paragraph is focused on a source.** This can occur in any type of assignment. Perhaps an author makes an interesting argument or employs a useful technique and you'd like to consider it in some detail. If you are going to write 200 words about a source, then it probably deserves an hour or two of your time in which you read and make notes. (However, we caution against producing your assignments by summarizing one source per paragraph. As we detail later, often synthesis is a better approach.)

3. **A sentence or two is focused on a source.** This is common and can occur in any assignment type. For example, when reviewing literature, sometimes you'll make a claim and provide several citations to support the claim (see Example 7.2 for instances of this). This might be the only time you mention a particular source. The same occurs in essays whose task is to explore the complexities of a subject (essays can be similar to literature reviews). When reading and making notes on such sources, it's enough to identify and record the central argument or finding and maybe one or two other key points that are useful for your assignment and your brief thoughts about how the information is useful. This can be done in 15 or 20 minutes or even less.

What should my notes look like?

There are no rules about what your notes should look like. After all, you aren't marked on your notes. You can make notes in the following broad ways:

- You can make notes in the margin of a source, either by hand or electronically.
- You can handwrite notes.
- You can type notes by using a program like Word.
- You can use a note-making app or software (there are many).
- You can draw your notes (for example, you could make a 'mind map').

Box 6.1 provides the details of the information you should usually include in your notes.

Box 6.1   Key information to include in your notes

1. **The bibliographical details of your source.** In most instances (if you are handwriting or typing your notes or using an app), you should begin by recording the full bibliographical details of your source. You will need this information to cite the source correctly, and it can be time-consuming to find it after you've written your assignment.

2. **The page number(s) of relevant information.** When you come across something relevant, note the page number(s). If you use the information, you'll need to include the page number in the in-text citation. (This is when you acknowledge a source in the body of an assignment.)

3. **The relevant information from your source.** This might be a quotation (the exact words), a summary or a paraphrase. It is sometimes better to quote directly in your notes so that no information is lost or inadvertently modified.

4. **Your thoughts about how the information is useful for you.** Respond to at least some of the following questions about the source:
   - Does the source introduce you to a new topic for discussion?
   - Does it mention useful facts, techniques, arguments, opinions, concepts, theories or figures?
   - How is the information similar to or different from the information in other sources?
   - What is your opinion about the information?
   - How can the information be combined with the information in other sources?
   - Where should the information appear in your assignment?
   - Does the source mention aspects of your topic that you'd like to explore further?

5. **Optional: A heading that briefly indicates the content of the note.** Headings within your notes can help immensely when reviewing your notes.

Example 6.1 illustrates what your typed notes might look like (handwritten notes would be similar). We are imagining that we are responding to the question, 'What are the problems with the current use of statistics and how can these be solved?' Our source is an article by McShane and Gelman, 'Abandon statistical significance' (2017). If you are not familiar with statistical significance, don't worry, it's not very complicated. The rough idea is that in a study, such as an investigation into whether a new drug reduces the risk of an infection, if the result is statistically significant, then the drug works. 'P values' are used to establish whether a result is statistically significant. Values range between 0 and 1, and the closer to 0, the more likely a finding is statistically significant. Often, researchers decide that the value should be less than 0.05 for an effect to be claimed.

Example 6.1   An example of notes in relation to an article

If you like, you can treat this example as an activity. Simply make your own notes about the article in response to the question, 'What are the problems with the current use of statistics and how can these be solved?' Then you can look over our notes and the accompanying annotations.

The article: 'Abandon statistical significance' by McShane and Gelman (2017)

In many fields, decisions about whether to publish an empirical finding, pursue a line of research or enact a policy are considered only when results are 'statistically significant', defined as having a P value (or similar metric) that falls below some pre-specified threshold. This approach is called null hypothesis significance testing (NHST). It encourages researchers to investigate so many paths in their analyses that whatever appears in papers is an unrepresentative selection of the data.

Worse, NHST is often taken to mean that any data can be used to decide between two inverse claims: either 'an effect' that posits a relationship between, say, a treatment and an outcome (typically the favoured hypothesis) or 'no effect' (defined as the null hypothesis).

In practice, this often amounts to uncertainty laundering. Any study, no matter how poorly designed and conducted, can lead to statistical significance and thus a declaration of truth or falsity. NHST was supposed to protect researchers from over-interpreting noisy data. Now it has the opposite effect.

This year has seen a debate about whether tightening the threshold for statistical significance would improve science. More than 150 researchers have weighed in. We think improvements will come not from tighter thresholds, but from dropping them altogether. We have no desire to ban P values. Instead, we wish them to be considered as just one piece of evidence among many, along with prior knowledge, plausibility of mechanism, study design and data quality, real-world costs and benefits, and other factors. For more, see our article with David Gal at the University of Illinois at Chicago, Christian Robert at the University of Paris-Dauphine and Jennifer Tackett at Northwestern University.

For example, consider a claim, published in a leading psychology journal in 2011, that a single exposure to the US flag shifts support towards the Republican Party for up to eight months. In our view, this finding has no backing from political-science theory or polling data; the reported effect is implausibly large and long-lasting; the sample sizes were small and non-representative; and the measurements (for example, those of voting and political ideology) were noisy. Although the authors stand by their findings, we argue that their P values provide very little information.

Statistical-significance thresholds are perhaps useful under certain conditions: when effects are large and vary little under the conditions being studied and when variables can be measured accurately. This may well describe the experiments for which NHST and canonical statistical methods were developed, such as agricultural trials in the 1920s and 1930s examining how various fertilizers affected crop yields. Nowadays, however, in areas ranging from policy analysis to biomedicine, changes tend to be small, situation-dependent and difficult to measure. For example, in nutrition studies, it can be a challenge to get accurate reporting of dietary choices and health outcomes.

Open-science practices can benefit science by making it more difficult for researchers to make overly strong claims from noisy data, but cannot by themselves compensate for poor experiments. Real advances will require researchers to make predictions more capable of probing their theories and invest in more precise measurements featuring, in many cases, within-person comparisons.

A crucial step is to move beyond the alchemy of binary statements about 'an effect' or 'no effect' with only a P value dividing them. Instead, researchers must accept uncertainty and embrace variation under different circumstances.

Our notes

Our heading highlights what we think is the most useful aspect of the quotation.

Great description of 'uncertainty laundering'—useful concept

p. 558: 'It [null hypothesis significance testing] encourages researchers to investigate so many paths in their analyses that whatever appears in papers is an unrepresentative selection of the data.... [T]his often amounts to uncertainty laundering. Any study, no matter how poorly designed and conducted, can lead to statistical significance and thus a declaration of truth or falsity. NHST was supposed to protect researchers from over-interpreting noisy data. Now it has the opposite effect.'

We respond to the quotation from the point of view of the question.

We clarify our understanding of 'uncertainty laundering'.

Our thoughts: These remarks are great. They clarify several problems with statistics: (P1) The first problem is 'uncertainty laundering'. 'Uncertainty laundering' refers to combing through data until one finds statistical significance. A related problem with statistics is that (P2) poorly designed studies can provide statistical significance. A related problem: (P3) NHST was once thought of as a

We record our general positive evaluation.

This signposting both identifies and begins to help us organize topics for discussion.

cure for bad research and now is part of the problem. This potentially shows deeper problems: (P4) Scientists aren't being trained properly and probably also (P5) the culture of institutions, journals, and so on is not right: scientists are being rewarded for producing attractive results (statistically significant results), not for the rigorous nature of their work. We should explore these aspects further. In regard to solutions, it follows from the arguments of McShane and Gelman that (S1) the problems with statistics can't be fixed just with a statistical solution. Rather, (S2) Better norms and training are needed – this would include modifications and training in experiment design and analysis techniques. (S3) Even a change in the culture of the research community might be needed.

Useful critique of 'open-science practices'

p. 558: 'Open-science practices can benefit science by making it more difficult for researchers to make overly strong claims from noisy data, but cannot by themselves compensate for poor experiments.'

Our thoughts: Here again, we have the problem that the issue is not statistics themselves but poor experiment design (P2 above). The authors mention an interesting solution: (S4) open science practices. We could find other researchers who advocate this approach. The authors' critique of open science practices leads us back to the problems and solutions discussed above.

Aspects of the notes we have just produced could also have been drawn. Given that the question asks about problems and solutions, it makes sense that our drawing (see Figure 6.1) is structured in the same way (we focus on problems for the sake of brevity). As you'll see, one advantage of the graphical method is that you can clearly show levels of abstraction; that is, you can indicate when, say, one problem sits within a broader problem. As we went through the process of mapping the five problems we identified (three came from McShane and Gelman and two were our own extrapolations from McShane and Gelman's discussion), we found that at the broadest level there is the problem with research culture. Within that, there is the problem that NHST is not being used appropriately, and within that, there are the specific problems of training, experiment design and analysis techniques, all of which overlap.

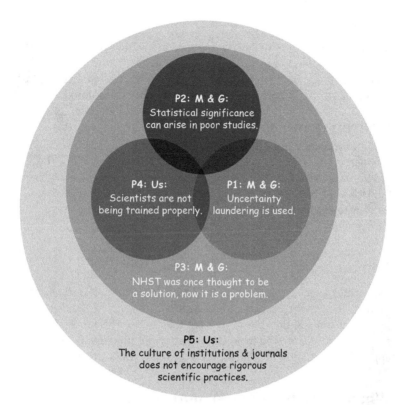

Figure 6.1   A mind map of five problems with the current use of statistics

The benefits of making digital notes: accessibility, speed, searchability, reference assistance

Although handwriting notes is possible, making notes digitally, whether using Word documents or an app, has several benefits.

Accessibility

If your notes are digital, whether they are stored on a thumb drive or in the cloud, then you can access them anywhere: you don't have to carry around reams of paper with you.

Speed

Digital notes are faster to produce than written notes. Also, you can copy and paste passages from your sources into your notes and from your notes into your assignments.

Searchability

The greatest benefit of digital notes is the ease with which you can find information within them. So long as you remember a word or a phrase from a quotation or in your own ideas, you can use a find function ('Ctrl + F' for PCs and 'Command + F' for Macs) to locate the information.

Referencing assistance

Whether you are using a program like Word or a note-making app, you can load in the bibliographical details of your sources as you go. The program can then help you with in-text citations and produce a reference list. However, be aware that you might have to change some of the settings to ensure that the format is consistent with the assignment requirements.

Combining note-making techniques

Many researchers combine note-making techniques. For less significant sources, they might just make a few electronic notes on a PDF. For more significant sources, they might type out their notes. This is because doing so helps them to develop their ideas. They might then use a graphical approach to organize their ideas. We'll say more about this in Chapter 9.

When it's ok not to make notes

In regard to your assignments, note-making is most useful early on when you are working out what you should discuss, developing your ideas and thinking about how you will organize your ideas. As we'll explain in Chapter 9, once you've written a substantial portion of your assignment, you can simply insert the information you read and your thoughts about it directly into your writing without wasting time making notes.

Conclusion

Making useful notes is one of the great challenges of studying at university. You'll always be trying to strike a balance between making too many notes and not making enough. It will only be with practice that you gain a good sense of how you can best use your notes to enrich your studies, whether this be preparing for class or producing your assignments. Notes are most successful when you record not just the words of others but indicate how the information is useful for you.

Reading to Work Out What a Source Is Generally About

Introduction

As we mentioned in Chapter 1, academic sources are 'bumpy' not 'smooth'. In a smooth source, like a novel, all the words are equally important: if you skip bits, you'll quickly become lost. Because of this, the way to read a novel is to start at the beginning and read every word until you get to the end. In a 'bumpy' source, like an academic article, some words are more important than others and these are the words you should focus on if you want to gain a general sense of what the source is about. For many sources, the most important words are those that clarify the problem being addressed and the solution.

In this chapter, we'll begin by explaining when reading for the bumps is useful and say a few words about how academic articles in particular are structured. We'll then introduce six questions you should ask of any source you are exploring. For academic articles, usually the questions can be answered by reading the articles' abstracts, introductions and conclusions. Finally, we'll outline the next step you can take: 'overviewing'. This 'second pass' at a source will allow you to deepen your understanding of it.

When it is useful to read for the 'bumps'

Reading for the bumps is most useful if you want to dedicate only 10 or 20 minutes to a source. This will be the case when:

- **you are completing your set readings.** Realistically, you won't have the 10 or even 20 hours necessary to read every word of your set readings each week. Even if you did have the time, reading every word would likely be counterproductive. However, you'll certainly be able to extract the key information from several sources in an hour or two; by doing this, you'll be well prepared for your classes and you'll be laying the foundations for producing successful assignments.

- **you are reading broadly in the early stages of an assignment.** Reading for the bumps will help you work out whether a source is relevant and deserves more attention. It will also introduce you to potentially useful topics for discussion. (See the discussion of the assignment-producing process in Chapter 9.)
- **you are reading to understand your field.** Reading for the bumps in conjunction with thinking about your field (see Box 13.1) will help you to rapidly improve your understanding of your field. This understanding will benefit you throughout your studies and subsequent career.

The different structures of sources: scientific versus essayistic structures

Before you search for key information in a source, it's useful to understand the type of source you are dealing with and how this affects the structure of the source – this will help you search for information more effectively. Although there is immense variety in how academic sources are structured, we can distinguish between the more standardized 'scientific' structures and the less standardized 'essayistic' structures.

The fundamental difference between a scientific or empirical approach to solving problems and an essayistic approach is that, in the former, the researcher produces their own evidence by conducting a study whereas, in the latter, evidence is drawn from existing sources.

Typically, the standard scientific structure mimics the problem-solving process. Namely, the problem is introduced and placed in its broader context, the method for solving the problem is explained, the data that were gathered are meaningfully presented and discussed, and finally the solution is given (see Box 7.1 for more details).

In contrast, there is no standard structure for essayistic work. Notably, for essayistic writing, introductions often do more than introductions in scientific work. You will commonly see not just the subject and problem introduced and perhaps an overview of the method used, but the solution and details of how the argument will be developed or structured. For scientific work, the solution doesn't appear until the conclusion.

An interesting overlap between the two forms is that the literature review section in the scientific structure is often essayistic in nature. This is because both literature reviews and essayistic sources are often concerned with exploring the complexities of a subject.

Box 7.1   The standard 'scientific' structure

Introduction/literature review
- The subject is introduced.
- The current state of knowledge about the subject is reviewed (this is referred to as a 'literature review').
- The specific problem and accompanying aim are stated.
- There may be an overview of the method used to gather data.
- Sometimes, a hypothesis is articulated. A hypothesis is a prediction that can be tested that will allow the problem to be resolved.

Method
- The method for gathering data (evidence) is explained.

Results
- The collected data are presented in a meaningful manner.

Discussion
- The significance of the results is discussed. This usually involves exploring the results in relation to the current state of knowledge as presented in the literature review.

Conclusion
- There is a definitive statement about what was achieved in relation to the hypothesis (if there was one) and the original problem. In short, it provides the solution (if, indeed, a solution was obtained).
- Limitations of the study are considered.
- Directions for future research are suggested.

The 'first pass': six questions to help you work out what a source is about

Before you even consider reading a source from beginning to end, come up with answers to the questions listed in Box 7.2. You should be able to answer these questions by reading the title, abstract (an abstract is a summary of an article that appears at the start), the introduction and perhaps also the conclusion. We explain each of the questions after the box.

Well-written sources will clearly and systematically address these questions. For others, you might need to read between the lines a little. Also, as mentioned, these elements won't always appear in the same places for different sources. For example, when a scientific structure is used, often key information in the introduction is in the first and last paragraphs; this is because the middle paragraphs constitute the literature review (see Example 7.2).

Box 7.2   Reading for the 'bumps': six questions that will help you work out what a source is about

1. To which **subject** does the source contribute?

2. What **problem** is being addressed?

3. Why are the subject and problem **significant**?

4. What **method** is used to solve the problem and why is it **appropriate**?

5. What is the **solution**?

6. Is there any mention of significant **concepts**, **theories**, **debates** or **people** in the field?

---

1. Usually, the **subject** is introduced in the title and first line of the abstract or introduction. By identifying the subject to which the source contributes, you'll know broadly what the source is about but also where to 'file' the information in the source. Usually, the subject is broader than the problem being addressed. For example, an article in Optometry might be concerned with the problem of contact lens discomfort in relation to the tear lipid layer (you don't need to know what this is!), but the problem sits – obviously – within the broader subject of contact lens comfort.

2. The **problem** being addressed by the source is sometimes introduced in the title or first sentence or two of the abstract or introduction. However, sometimes the problem is announced only after there has been an overview of the subject. You need to be clear about the problem because, in most cases, the entire source will be committed to solving this problem, so if you are not clear about it, the rest of the source won't make much sense. Remember, problems can be precisely defined or more open-ended. Precisely defined problems include questions such as how do we address a social injustice, how can a medical procedure be improved, how can a certain structure be better built and also activities such as describing a new organism. Open-ended problems often involve exploration; for example, we might not know what happens when we shoot a certain laser at a certain material. Problem statements can be transformed into research questions or aims and, in scientific research,

can be further refined as hypotheses. In scientific sources, hypotheses usually appear at the end of an introduction, just before the method section. Here are examples of the way phrasing changes for a problem statement, a question, an aim and a hypothesis.

- Problem statement: 'Drug X effectively treats the condition Y, but it has dangerous side effects. It is possible that modifying drug X by doing Z will reduce these side effects, but to date, this has not been attempted.'
- Question: 'Can drug X be modified by doing Z to reduce its dangerous side effects?'
- Aim: 'The study aims to determine whether doing Z to drug X will reduce its dangerous side effects.'
- Hypothesis: 'If we do Z to drug X, then the dangerous side effects of X will be reduced.'

3. The **significance** of the subject and problem is usually mentioned directly after each is introduced. Significance is important because, in a world of limited resources (money and time), we always want to know why a subject and problem deserve attention.
4. Remarks about **method** can appear in titles and usually appear in abstracts. In introductions, they can be found in different places. Understanding the method used to solve the problem will help you determine whether the solution is credible. For scientific work, method refers to the techniques used to gather evidence. For essayistic work, method can refer to how an argument is developed.
5. As mentioned, the **solution** to the problem often appears in the introduction of essayistic sources but only in the conclusion of scientific sources. It can also sometimes appear in the title and abstract. Even if all you take away from a source is a sense of the problem being addressed and the proposed solution, you will have learned something valuable. If you did this for 20 sources (which you can do very quickly), you will rapidly gain a strong understanding of your subject and broader field.
6. **Concepts, theories, debates** and **people** can be mentioned at any time in abstracts, introductions and conclusions. Keep an eye out for them and look them up if you need further information. As we discuss in Chapter 13, being aware of such things will help you to become more familiar with your field. And to do well in your assignments, it helps to include them.

And remember, you should always think about whether you agree with any claim being made and how the source might be useful for your assignment.

Worked examples of how to read for the bumps

We'll now present two worked examples: one from an 'essayistic' article and the other from a 'scientific' article.

Example 7.1 reproduces a paragraph from the introduction to the article, 'Silent slapstick film as ritualized clowning: the example of Charlie Chaplin' by James Caron (2006). The article, which is essayistic in nature and thus doesn't follow a standard structure, is about the function of slapstick – or physical – comedy. You'll see that the introduction addresses each of the six questions. (If you are not familiar with Charlie Chaplin, you'll be able to find excerpts of many of his movies on YouTube.)

Example 7.1   Reading for the bumps in an essayistic introduction

1. Subject.
6. Concept. It is useful to know what 'slapstick' is.

3. Significance of subject.

2. Problem. The problem is how to understand slapstick.

4. Method. Caron explains what he will analyze.

5. Solution. Slapstick is a form of 'ritual clowning'. Some of the details of the solution appear in the sentences that follow.

Slapstick may be the most popular type of comic art ever developed within the western comic tradition. [....] Slapstick thus provides a compelling subject for analysis. No doubt slapstick could be fertile ground, for example, on which to speculate about the complex dynamic between the representation of physical pain and the gut response of laughter. This essay, however, will explore another way to understand it, one that rests on a comparison with a well-documented behavior in traditional, non-western societies that anthropologists call ritual or sacred clowning. Examples taken from the short silent films of Charles Chaplin, specifically the two-reelers he made for Mutual Films in 1916 and 1917, will suggest that slapstick can be usefully understood as a quasi-ritualized and socially-sanctioned expression of proscribed behavior. In addition to arguing that basic elements of slapstick symbolically transgress ideal behavior, the essay will also suggest how the experience of movie-watching in modern western societies approximates the experience of a village-wide audience watching ritual clowning in traditional non-western societies. Viewing Chaplin's silent slapstick clowning performances with an audience in a movie theatre has the potential to create the sense of communitas that Victor Turner (1969) argues is part of ritual. Finally, as is the case in the ritual clowning of traditional non-western societies, slapstick clowning potentially subverts as well as conserves the norms of western societies.

3. Significance of subject. Slapstick is the most popular type of comic art; thus, it is worthy of analysis.

4. Method and appropriateness. The method is comparing slapstick with 'ritual clowning'. This method is appropriate because ritual clowning is 'well-documented'.
6. Concept. Ritual or sacred clowning.

6. We hear about the significant concept 'communitas' and the significant person, Victor Turner.

You might have already noticed that, when you read for the bumps, you need to read sentences and paragraphs several times. This is entirely appropriate and indeed it is evidence that you are being an active, not a passive, reader! Do you see how different academic reading is from reading novels, where you read every word once? And do you see that you don't need to be a fast reader to be an effective reader?

Example 7.2 is drawn from a scientific article: 'Conservation tillage and organic farming reduce soil erosion' by Seitz, Goebes, Puerta, et al. (2019). It reproduces the introduction and the first paragraph from the conclusion. The example is longer than the previous example because, as is often the case in scientific publications, the introduction contains a literature review. Given this, a bit more work will be needed to find the relevant 'bumps'. As you'll see, the article begins by introducing a broad subject and problem: soil erosion. Then, in the literature review, it introduces the dimensions of the problem that it wants to study: conventional farming, organic farming and conservation tillage. This allows the article to articulate the specific problem it will address: the effects of reduced tillage, organic farming and conventional farming on soil erosion.

Example 7.2   Reading for the bumps in a scientific introduction

1 & 2. Subject of the article and also the broad problem being addressed. Details of the broad problem follow.

Soil erosion is a major environmental problem with severe impacts on terrestrial and fluvial ecosystems (Smith et al., 2016). Verheijen et al. (2009) indicated that 3–40 t ha-1 of soil material is eroded in Europe every year, whereas mean soil formation rates do not exceed 0.3–1.4 t ha-1. It is well established that agricultural practices greatly influence soil erosion (Montgomery, 2007). In particular, the intensification of cultivation after World War II led to increased soil losses (Matson, 1997). In this context,

2. Significance.

1. Subject. The first of the three sub-subjects of the article is introduced: conventional farming strategies.

conventional farming strategies have drawn criticism (Gomiero, 2013), because they often lead to diminished topsoil depth, degraded soil structure, soil compaction, losses of soil organic matter (SOM), and nutrient depletion (Morgan, 2005). As a consequence, crop yields can be reduced and fields rendered unproductive over the long term (Bünemann et al., 2018).

1. Subject. The second of the three sub-subjects is introduced: organic farming.

Besides conventional farming systems, alternative strategies like organic farming are of growing interest (Gomiero et al., 2011a; Reganold and Wachter, 2016). Even if "organic farming" appears to be a broadly used term, it is regulated by different certifying institutional bodies and generally relies on crop rotation, absence of synthetic agrochemicals, and weed control without herbicides (Gomiero et al., 2011b). Although organic farming practices often lead to reduced crop yields (Ponisio et al., 2014; Wittwer et al., 2017), they can increase soil fertility and are associated with increased biological diversity (Hole et al., 2005; Verbruggen et al., 2010; Knapp and van der Heijden, 2018). Furthermore, organic farming practices generally enhance soil surface cover (Reganold et al., 1987) and improve soil structure by stabilizing soil aggregation (Erhart and Hartl, 2009). Several studies showed higher SOM contents in the topsoil layer on arable land under organic farming than conventional land use, which is a factor that can positively affect soil stabilization (Six et al., 2000a; Ghabbour et al., 2017).

3. Significance.

Furthermore, studies showed that organic farming has the potential to diminish soil erosion (Erhart and Hartl, 2009). Most of those studies are based on models such as the Universal Soil Loss Equation (USLE, empirical) or the Water Erosion Prediction Project (WEPP, process-based) (Lockeretz et al., 1981; Reganold, 1988; Auerswald et al., 2003; Pacini et al., 2003; Arnhold et al., 2014). Some studies indirectly assessed soil erosion by evaluating topsoil thickness (Reganold et al., 1987), soil erodibility (Fleming et al., 1997; Siegrist et al., 1998; Kuhn et al., 2012), aggregate stability (Mulla et al., 1992; Pulleman et al., 2003), or nutrients in runoff of farm drainage systems (Eltun et al., 2002) and one study directly assessed soil erosion in organically versus conventionally managed plots (Weilgart Patten, 1982) using the Alutin rill method. Even if it can be stated that erosion models have originally been calibrated with field data, there is a general lack of experimental in situ measurements to compare organic farming systems (Gomiero, 2013). In particular, experimental research with comparable conditions (e.g., in soil type and texture) for both organic and conventional

2. Problem. An aspect of the specific problem is introduced.

treatments is scarce (Reganold, 1988; Auerswald et al., 2003).

A number of studies revealed that conservation tillage (any tillage system that maintains at least 30% of cover on the soil surface, e.g., reduced or no tillage, cf. Soil Science Society of America, 2008) decreases soil erosion and improves soil structure (Six et al., 2000b; Zhang et al., 2007; Erhart and Hartl, 2009), but might also increase soil compaction in organic farming (Peigné et al., 2018). The advantage of reduced or no tillage systems is a higher soil surface cover throughout the year and better protection of soil structure or structure-forming soil organisms such as earthworms (Mikha and Rice, 2004; Blanco-Canqui and Lal, 2008). The benefits of these practices increase further when combined with diverse crop rotation (Pittelkow et al., 2015) and permanent soil cover to protect topsoils against particle detachment (Durán Zuazo and Rodríguez Pleguezuelo, 2008; Goebes et al., 2014). Reduced tillage does not abandon all mechanical operations for seedbed preparation, but minimizes tillage operations to the smallest frequency (e.g., for weed control in organic farming) necessary to guarantee crop growth (Soil Science Society of America, 2008). There is an increasing interest to apply conservation tillage practices under organic conditions (Armengot et al., 2015; Cooper et al., 2016), but to our knowledge, the impact of organic farming in combination with reduced tillage on soil erosion has not yet been tested. Moreover, it is still unclear how conservation or no tillage under conventional conditions compares to tilled organic systems. Thus, research on this topic is important to evaluate and potentially improve soil erosion control in different farming systems (Hösl and Strauss, 2016).

This study investigated soil erosion rates under simulated heavy rainfall events in situ in the Swiss Farming System and Tillage experiment (FAST, Prechsl et al., 2017; Wittwer et al., 2017; Hartman et al., 2018), a replicated and randomized field experiment with four major arable cropping systems (organic–intensive tillage, organic–reduced tillage, conventional–intensive tillage,

Margin notes (right):

1 & 6. Subject and Concept. The third of the three sub-subjects is introduced: conservation tillage.

2. Problem. We finally see all the dimensions of the specific problem to be addressed by the study.

3. Significance.

Margin notes (left):

4. Method and appropriateness. We are provided with an overview of the method of the study; namely, the four conditions to be studied are outlined. The appropriateness of the method is clearly addressed: the authors argue that the method allows cropping systems to be compared without confounding factors and also state that the method has been successfully used in other studies.

conventional–no tillage). Hence, we could compare these cropping systems directly without confounding factors such as differences in soil type, crop type, or crop rotation history. A portable rainfall simulator was used to dose precipitation over micro-scale runoff plots (ROP) in the field (Fig. 1). Subsequently, sediment delivery after simulated rainfall events was collected. This method has proven reliable in rough terrain conditions and is highly suitable to measure interrill soil erosion in replicated field experiments (Seitz, 2015).

We hypothesized that:

2. Problem. The hypotheses are proposed solutions to the problem. They will be tested in the study.

1. Organic farming reduces soil erosion when compared to conventional farming systems, as a consequence of higher soil surface cover and SOM content under organic farming.

2. A reduction of tillage intensity in organic farming further reduces soil erosion compared to intensive tillage practices.

First paragraph from the conclusion

This study enabled ranking four different arable cropping systems regarding soil erosion and showed for the first time in situ that the application of reduced tillage in organic farming can further decrease sediment delivery. **5. Solution.** Thus, it appears to be a major improvement for soil erosion control in organic farming systems. The experiment demonstrated that reduced soil erosion in organic agriculture compared to conventional agriculture was mainly driven by soil surface cover and SOM. Additionally, this work showed that a living plant cover from weeds can reduce soil erosion more effectively compared to dead plant residues in conventional, no-tillage systems.

5. Solution. Details of the solution are presented.

Note the general structure of the introduction in Example 7.2; many scientific articles employ a similar structure:

1. Subject and broad problem are introduced.
2. Significance is indicated.
3. Dimensions of the problem to be studied are clarified.

4. Specific problem is articulated.
5. Overview of method and its appropriateness are presented.
6. Hypotheses are stated.

ACTIVITY 7.1

Reading for the 'bumps' in an abstract

Below is an abstract for the article 'Diversification, intensification and specialization: changing land use in Western Africa from 1800 BC to AD 1500' by Kay et al. (2019). Try to find answers to each of the six questions in Box 7.2 (don't worry about Question 6).

The abstract

Many societal and environmental changes occurred between the 2nd millennium BC and the middle of the 2nd millennium AD in western Africa. Key amongst these were changes in land use due to the spread and development of agricultural strategies, which may have had widespread consequences for the climate, hydrology, biodiversity, and ecosystem services of the region. Quantification of these land-use influences and potential feedbacks between human and natural systems is controversial however, in part because the archaeological and historical record is highly fragmented in time and space. To improve our understanding of how humans contributed to the development of African landscapes, we developed an atlas of land use practices in western Africa for nine time-windows over the period 1800 BC–AD 1500. The maps are based on a broad synthesis of archaeological, archaeobotanical, archaeozoological, historical, linguistic, genetic, and ethnographic data, and present land use in 12 basic categories. The main differences between categories is the relative reliance on, and variety of, domesticated plant and animal species utilized, and the energy invested in cultivating or keeping them. The maps highlight the irregular and frequently non-linear trajectory of land-use change in the prehistory of western Africa. Representing an original attempt to produce rigorous spatial synthesis from diverse sources, the atlas will be useful for a range of studies of human–environment interactions in the past, and highlight major spatial and temporal gaps in data that may guide future field studies.

The 'second pass': overviewing

Reading for the bumps will have given you a good sense of what the source is about. Having extracted the key information from it, you could now happily move on to another source, or, if you like, you could explore the source in more detail. To use the analogy of a tree, in answering the six questions, you have been focusing on the trunk of the tree. By 'overviewing', you'll be casting your eyes upwards towards the main branches. The strategies for overviewing are outlined in Box 7.3.

Box 7.3   Four strategies for 'overviewing' a source

1. Get a sense of the **general structure** of the source. Read all the section headings (if the source is an article) or the contents pages (if the source is a book). Think about how these headings relate to the six questions from Box 7.1; specifically, think about how the solution to the problem is developed.

2. If you are dealing with a shorter source like an article, read the first sentence or two in each paragraph. These **topic sentences** usually indicate what the paragraph will discuss. If a topic sentence is appealing, read more of the paragraph. If you are dealing with a book, read the first paragraph from each of the chapters.

3. Read any **conclusions** you haven't yet read, such as those that might appear at the end of sections or chapters.

4. Determine whether any additional **concepts**, **theories**, **debates** or **significant people** are mentioned.

In Example 7.3, we return to Caron's article, 'Silent slapstick film as ritualized clowning: the example of Charlie Chaplin'. The article is around 5000 words. It has no headings, so we can't use overviewing strategy 1. However, strategies 2 to 4 are doable. We ensured we spent only 15 minutes looking over the topic sentences, reading a few of the more interesting paragraphs, identifying theories and concepts, and reading the conclusion. In the example, we explain part of our reading experience. The left column identifies which paragraph we are concerned with (we start with the third paragraph as the first two are the introduction) and includes the significant topic sentences. The right column presents our thoughts. Don't worry if a comment doesn't make sense; the point is to understand the process we used. It will be useful for you to overview this article as an activity before studying our experience (see Activity 7.3).

Overviewing practice

Locate Caron's 2006 article, 'Silent slapstick film as ritualized clowning: the example of Charlie Chaplin'. Read it using the overviewing strategies in Box 7.3. Compare your experience with ours in Example 7.3. This activity will also be useful if you haven't yet tried to access academic articles: use it as an opportunity to familiarize yourself with Google Scholar or your university library.

Example 7.3   Our experience of overviewing Caron's article

Paragraph and significant sentences	Our thoughts
3rd First sentence: 'Ritual clowning is a wide-spread comic phenomenon, appearing in particular in Native American and Polynesian societies.'	'Ritual clowning' is clearly the central concept in the article. We decided we should read the rest of the paragraph to learn about the nature of ritual clowning. We learned from the concluding sentence that ritual clowning takes place in a sacred ceremonial setting and that the clown 'inverts all proper behavior'.
4th First sentence: 'An excellent example of ritual clowns comes from the Zuni Indian tribe...'	The article is moving from making a general point to providing an example. We skipped this paragraph.
5th First two sentences: 'The effects of the clown's licensed play can be described in terms that are at once socially and psychologically symbolic. The ritual transgressions of the clowns create "*communitas*," Victor Turner's term for a symbolic state of being in which the usual hierarchies of society are supplanted by a sense of communal unity where equality is the norm.'	The concept 'communitas' is again mentioned. Given that it was mentioned in the introduction, we decided to read the full paragraph. We also Googled 'Victor Turner'. The paragraph was very useful.

6th First sentence: 'If the functionalist interpretation of the Zuni example can be taken as a model for understanding ritual clowning, the following qualities are salient...'
Concluding sentence: 'Above all, ritual clowns facilitate the movement within a ritual occasion between what Turner calls structure and anti-structure, mediating antithetical states such as sacred/profane, rational/irrational, serious/ frivolous, adult/child.'

Noting that the paragraph summarized the characteristics of ritual clowning, we read it all. The words 'Above all' in the last sentence of the paragraph (the paragraph had only two sentences) indicated to us the importance of the information that followed. We learned about the tension between 'structure' (conservative forces) and 'anti-structure' (transformative or even anarchistic forces).

7th First two sentences: 'Chaplin's personae in his work for Mutual Films can function in a similar way for western audiences. While in traditional rituals the disruptive clowns embodying anti-structure are paired with figures representative of structure – shamans and gods for example – Chaplin's personae represent both structure and anti-structure.'

We noted that the first sentence of this paragraph performs the structural function of showing the transition from discussing ritual clowning to discussing Chaplin. The sentence also reminds us of the article's main argument. Seeing as this paragraph was clearly the start of a new section, we also read the second sentence and learned what we thought was the main argument for the section: Chaplin's personae represent both structure and anti-structure. We now had the sense that even though we weren't far into the article, we'd learned much of what the article had to say (this turned out to be correct).

8th–26th This long stretch of paragraphs provides details of the different aspects of society that are both subverted and upheld by 'Charlie'. Amongst the topics that are explored are normal adult behaviour, sexuality, work and the concept of progress.

Armed with the idea that Chaplin's personae are a mix of 'structure' and 'anti-structure', we found it easy to simply note each of the general points flagged in the topic sentences and skip the lengthy examples. We spent no more than a couple of minutes on these 19 paragraphs.

For the sake of brevity we abridge our analysis and jump to the end of the article

35th–36th First sentence of **35th:** 'If some merit exists to my claim that slapstick movies function in modern societies in a way that approaches ritual clowning in traditional societies, then one must also understand how deeply conservative is the laughter these comic analogues generate.'	We quickly recognized that these last two paragraphs remind us of the main argument made in the article: that slapstick performs a similar function in developed societies as ritual clowning in traditional societies. It provides a space for people to communally break the rules without ultimately disrupting society.

What can we say about the 'overviewing' experience? An important question is: what did we learn from 'overviewing' the article that we didn't already know from reading the introduction? The answer is, not that much: the overviewing revealed that the useful information is indeed contained in the introduction. The details and examples added depth but rarely moved into new territory. This certainly won't always be the case but will be when there is a thorough introduction.

Conclusion

In this chapter, we've suggested that you can gain a lot from a source without reading every word. Indeed, you may well gain more from a source if you don't read every word. This is because you'll be focusing on the 'bumps': the important pieces of information. It's all too easy to be a 'reading martyr' and fall into a 'reading trance' and let the words pass through your mind without taking them in.

Thinking about the bumps: the main point is that all sources, from the Sciences to the Humanities, are addressing a problem in one form or another. So, when reading, identify this problem and also why it's important, how it was solved and the solution itself. If you want to explore a source in more detail, you can determine its structure by reading headings or contents pages and the first sentences of all the paragraphs. Also, keep an eye out for significant concepts, theories, debates and people. By using such strategies, you'll be able to explore a good number of sources in a relatively short amount of time. You'll need to do this with your set readings but also in the early stages of your assignments when, ideally, you survey multiple sources.

8

Reading in Depth

On several occasions, we've mentioned the 'T' model of reading. In the T model, the horizontal part of the T refers to reading for breadth of understanding of a subject or a topic within the subject and the vertical part refers to reading for depth of understanding of one source. Much of the time, we've supported reading for breadth. This is because in most contexts you'll gain more from learning what ten sources say about a topic rather than carefully studying one source. However, in some instances, reading for depth is necessary. This occurs when an assignment requires you to explore a single source, or if, say, you are trying to understand a key work, as often occurs in research degrees in later years of study. For example, you might be studying Developmental Psychology and so decide to examine Piaget's *Structuralism*. Or you might be studying Sociology and you decide to examine Durkheim's *The Rules of Sociological Method*. The question we want to answer in this brief chapter is: how should you go about reading what are often challenging and lengthy works? There is no easy answer to this question; however, we suggest several useful approaches. The extended activity in Chapter 11 will allow you to practice some of the skills introduced in this chapter.

The central advice: read with a purpose

Before you read something in depth, be clear about why you are reading the work. There is usually more in a piece of writing than you will identify in even several readings. And you could study some works for a lifetime and continue to find new ideas; this is because they often contain many remarkable insights. Thus, you need to read with a *filter* in place so that you catch the information that will be useful for you. Your purpose or filter will come from either an assignment's guidelines or, if you are producing a dissertation, the project you are working on. In more detail:

- Sometimes you'll have a clear assignment question that tells you what to focus on while reading in depth. One such question is: 'Explain and assess Locke's account of sense perception'. Naturally, if responding to this question, when reading the relevant work, you would have the words 'sense perception' at the front of your mind. And given the question asks you to 'explain and assess', you'll not only be trying to understand Locke's account, you'll be asking yourself: 'do I agree?' The extended activity in Chapter 11 will give you the opportunity to read an article in depth with some specific purposes in mind.
- Other assignments are more open-ended in their instructions. Consider the following instructions for a critical review in the area of International Relations: 'Select two articles with differing perspectives that discuss an aspect of gender in an international context. Summarize the position of each text. Clarify how the positions of the two differ. Explain which position is the most compelling – you may decide that neither position is compelling and suggest a third position.' Even though you are required to select the topic and find relevant sources, what you will be doing in the assignment is very similar to the previous question about Locke: there will be a degree of explaining and a degree of assessing.
- If you are reading a key work as part of a dissertation, then be clear about the problem you are addressing in your research and hopefully also the various sub-problems or questions associated with this. This will provide you with an angle from which to approach the work.

Reading key sources: ease your way in by reading summaries, general analyses and secondary sources

When reading key sources, you can begin simply by reading the work and seeing how the ideas strike you. However, you can also ease yourself in by reading overviews of the work on websites like Wikipedia and, if they exist, in academic sources that introduce and critique the work. For example, if you were starting to study Nietzsche, you could read the Wikipedia page about him and you could also survey *The Oxford Handbook of Nietzsche* or *A Companion to Nietzsche.*

There are pros and cons both for going straight to the work itself and for easing yourself in through secondary sources. If you begin by reading the work unassisted, the benefit is that your own critical faculties will not be swayed by what others have said. The cons are that you might find the work to be impenetrable, as can occur with more philosophical or theoretical works; and you might waste time reading less important aspects of the work: perhaps the work is significant because of one particular section.

There are several benefits for beginning by reading overviews and critiques:

- Most obviously, you'll learn what, generally, the work is about. This will include learning about the topics it explores, its position on these topics and the most significant sections of the work.
- You'll also benefit greatly from understanding why the work is so highly regarded. In other words, you'll benefit from understanding the work's place in the broader field it sits within; Wikipedia is especially good for providing this information, as you can follow the links to discussions of the broader field. When you eventually read the work itself, various sections will jump out at you because you'll already have a sense of aspects of the work that have had an impact on the field.
- If you begin by learning what others say about a work, you'll be filled with conjectures about the work that you can then *test* as you yourself read the work. In other words, don't trust what others say about the work; rather, as you read, ask yourself whether they are correct.

⎣→this would help to develop your own opinion

Begin by reading for the bumps and overviewing

Even when the goal is to carefully read every word of a source, begin by reading for the 'bumps' as outlined in the previous chapter. So, be clear about, amongst other things, the problem being addressed, its significance and the solution. And get a sense of the structure of the work by reading chapter or section titles (or both) and, for shorter works, at least some topic sentences.

Read critically

When reading in depth, even when not explicitly directed by assignment guidelines, you should be critical of what you read. While we'll say more about critical reading in later chapters, you can have these broad questions in mind:

CRITICAL READING QUESTIONS

- Is the subject being explored worthy of exploration?
- Are the specific problems being addressed worthy of exploration?
- Are the methods used appropriate?
- Are individual claims sufficiently supported by evidence? What is the nature and quality of the evidence?
- How does the work compare with other works? Do similarities add weight to what is presented? How can differences be resolved? Is one perspective superior to another?
- How can the information in the source be usefully combined with other information?
- Can I build upon what I read?

Reread

Whether you are critiquing an article for an assignment or trying to understand a key work, it's often not until the second or third reading that you really begin to understand the details of what's being discussed. This is assisted by taking breaks of at least a day or two between readings. During this break, you'll continue to think about the source and this will help you immeasurably when you return to it.

Make notes

If you are reading for an assignment, then the aspects of a source about which you make notes will be guided by the assignment question. It is often enough to make notes in the margin of a source about interesting passages so that when you reread the work your attention is drawn to these passages and you are reminded of your own thoughts. Having surveyed the work a couple of times, you'll then be in a better place to make more substantial notes – if needed – because you'll have a good sense of which aspects are most useful for you.

A note about the challenges of reading theory or philosophy

Some writing, especially on theory and philosophy, can be extremely technical, even for seasoned academics. This is true of older works, such as the writings of Kant or Hegel, but also of often-cited recent theorists such as Butler or Derrida. These works can be challenging for several reasons:

1. The writing is produced for people who are already knowledgeable about the field.

What you can do: Learn more about the field, starting with the types of problems the field is interested in, technical terms and debates.

2. The author is trying to accurately explore complex phenomena.

What you can do: Be patient. If you are being introduced to ideas you haven't thought about before, then you'll struggle with them the first time you encounter them. On your first reading, develop questions. Try to answer these questions when you reread.

3. The writing is not very good. The great problem with difficult writing is deciding whether the writing is challenging because it's deep or because it's poor. Some academic writing is unnecessarily dense, filled with jargon and vague.

What you can do: Read more secondary sources to understand what's being argued or possibly abandon studying the work and move on to something else.

Conclusion

Although you can often get through your studies simply by reading for breadth of understanding of your subjects, at times you'll likely have to read for depth. This can occur when a source is the focus of an assignment but also if you decide to study a seminal work to enrich your dissertation. As always, you'll benefit from reading with a purpose, whether this be dictated by assignment guidelines or your own project. You'll also likely benefit from reading secondary material about a work, if it exists. This will include learning about the work's place in the broader field. When reading the work itself, begin by reading for the 'bumps' and overviewing it before reading in more depth. Maintain a critical mindset throughout and make brief marginal or additional notes to guide you on subsequent readings. Produce more substantial notes only once you have a sense of how you'll use the work. Once again, we include an extended worked example in Chapter 11 that will allow you to practice some of these skills, in particular, reading a longer piece of writing with different purposes in mind.

9

The Assignment-Production Process: Reading, Planning and Writing

Introduction

Having explained in Chapters 7 and 8 how to read to understand what individual sources are about, we now move to the more complex process of reading for your assignments. In Assumption 7 in Chapter 1, we introduced the misconception that, to produce an assignment, first you read and then you write. Although it is true that the earlier stages of producing an assignment often include more reading than writing and this is reversed in the later stages, a strong assignment is often the outcome of moving backwards and forwards between reading and writing.

There is certainly no 'right' process. As with making notes, even the same person will modify their approach to an assignment depending on what they already know and how much time they have. However, the general strategy of reading around your topic and planning before you undertake more substantial reading and writing will be useful in most circumstances.

Although there are many types of assignments, in writing this chapter, we mostly have in mind essays and literature reviews. Essays are a common form of assessment in many disciplines, and literature reviews are present in studies and reports and also appear in most dissertations. Essays and literature reviews are similar in that both can require you to critically explore a range of topics in relation to a broader subject or problem. With this in mind, in this chapter, we'll be continuing our advice about how to read for breadth of understanding.

We'll begin with some words of encouragement (we know all too well that producing assignments is challenging!). We'll then provide an overview of the assignment-production process and explore each step in detail.

Some words of encouragement

Locating relevant sources, finding the useful information within them and then doing something worthwhile with the information is time-consuming and often difficult, even for experienced academics. One of the biggest challenges is that you'll read things that are not relevant and write things that you'll later delete. This is normal – even necessary. So, our advice is to be patient: don't worry if you can't figure out how to approach your assignment right away.

Also, for many students, it can take two or three years, if not more, to develop their reading and writing skills to a level where they are fully in control of them. By 'in control', we mean the student can move through the process with the confidence that if they follow the steps they'll achieve a good outcome every time. It also takes time to become familiar with your field of study, where this familiarity will help with things like being aware of significant debates and weighing different pieces of information. The steps we present in this chapter will help you better navigate the research process, but there's no substitute for the experience you'll gain from producing multiple assignments and reflecting on the process.

ACTIVITY 9.1

How do you produce your assignments?

Before reading this chapter, think about how you produce assignments. Answer the following questions:

1. How have you produced assignments in the past – or how do you produce assignments now?

2. Is your approach effective? If so, why? If not, why not?

3. Do you have any habits that waste time?

4. Are there any challenges you continue to encounter?

5. How could you improve the process you use?

The research process: the dialectical relationship between reading and writing

Before we explain the process itself, we'd like to introduce a technical term: 'dialectical' (which is an adjective, the noun is 'dialectic'). The term 'dialectical' might sound scary, but what it refers to is straightforward. In a dialectical relationship, there are two elements. In our case, they are reading and writing. The idea is that over time the two elements interact and ultimately come together to produce something valuable. For your assignments, you usually need to go back and forth between reading and writing a few times to produce a strong assignment. You'll start with general reading and writing (reading, for example, Wikipedia articles and planning) and move to specific reading and writing (reading academic articles and working on individual paragraphs). If you start by reading entire academic articles without having any idea what you are looking for (starting at Stage 5 in Box 9.1), then you'll struggle to extract useful information and waste time, and you might find it hard to write anything at all about what you read. But equally, if you try to write your full assignment without having read anything (starting at Stage 7), then you'll likely fail to write about significant topics and you'll have difficulty structuring your ideas.

The assignment-production process

Box 9.1 outlines the assignment-production process from a dialectical perspective. We explain the stages afterwards.

Box 9.1   A summary of the assignment-production process

Stage 1: Begin to establish topics for discussion: draw on what you've learned from class and set readings and what you already know.

Stage 2: Read generally to refine your topics for discussion: consult the internet.

Stage 3: Plan: transform your topics into a provisional 'tree diagram' or 'skeleton' of your assignment.

Stage 4: Do some rough-drafting: start to produce your paragraphs.

Stage 5: Find and read academic sources and make notes.

Stage 6: Refine your tree diagram.

Stage 7: Produce a solid draft.

Stage 8: Read opportunistically to find additional sources.

Stage 9: Revise (as much as possible) before submission.

After our discussion of the stages in the assignment-production process, we'll briefly illustrate Stages 1 and 3 so you get a sense of what starting out looks like. The synthesis example in Chapter 12 will illustrate one way to produce individual paragraphs.

Stage 1: Begin to establish topics for discussion: draw on what you've learned from class, set readings and what you already know

In a typical 1,000- to 2,000-word assignment, you'll be exploring two layers of complexity. The first layer is the topics you'll cover; the second is the complexities within each topic. In practical terms, the first layer is your different paragraphs and the second is what occurs in each paragraph. Given this, a good place to start an assignment is to work out what topics should populate the first layer and to begin to think about the details within them.

Although you could start by finding and surveying academic sources and hope that as you move through them you'll begin to identify relevant topics, you'll be better served by working out what you already know. This knowledge will come from what you've learned from your classes and set readings, and also from your existing knowledge.

What you should do at this stage

- Drawing on your classes, set readings and what you already know, write down all the possible topics, and perhaps also arguments, examples, concepts and so on, that might be relevant to your assignment. Don't worry at this stage if the information overlaps and if you can't work out what order to put it in.
- For each piece of information, include any sources you have come across that are potentially relevant. You don't need to say why they are relevant, but it will be useful if you can.
- If you have managed to identify discrete topics, in your notes, make each topic a heading and include details underneath. If you are drawing your notes, then you can make each topic into a bubble; this graphical method can make it easier to show the relationships between topics (see Chapter 6).
- If you are writing an essay, think about and note your general response to the question. This is usually referred to as your 'thesis'. However, you could do this at a later stage once you have a better sense of the subject.

Stage 2: Read generally to refine your topics for discussion: consult the internet

Once you've emptied your brain, it's time to look more widely to continue to determine what you could write about. You can do this by consulting the internet.

What you should do at this stage

- Using keywords from the assignment question and from the topics you've identified in Stage 1, do some Googling.
- Read anything you can find, from Wikipedia articles to quora.com and articles produced by news websites. You are doing this not to find material you'll directly include in your assignment but to continue to determine which topics you should discuss in your assignment and to learn about debates, specific arguments, examples, significant figures, sources, concepts and so on.
- Add what you find to your existing notes.
- If relevant, refine your thesis.

Stage 3: Plan: transform your topics into a provisional 'tree diagram' or 'skeleton' of your assignment

Once you've identified a range of topics and you are beginning to feel more confident about the dimensions of the problem you are addressing – once you have a sense of the issues that matter and some of their complexities – it's time to think about how you might structure your assignment. There is often great flexibility with how you can present your ideas. Given this, it will usually take a few drafts before you find the structure that works best for you. However, whatever structure you decide on should be able to be represented by a 'tree diagram' or 'skeleton'.

What you should do at this stage

- Identify discrete topics for discussion; this will involve grouping together closely related topics identified in Stages 1 and 2.
- You can also think about the level of abstraction that your topics belong to. Perhaps you can dedicate a paragraph to a topic, or perhaps the topic is just a detail in a paragraph on a broader topic.
- Try to come up with a logical order for discussing your topics. Depending on your assignment, this could involve considering pros then cons or establishing foundational points before moving on to secondary points or some other arrangement. You should be able to explain how each topic relates to the topics around it.

- Draw the 'tree diagram' or 'skeleton' of your structure. Once again, see the example later in the chapter.

Stage 4: Do some rough-drafting: start to produce your paragraphs

This stage is optional. If you feel that you have a good grasp of some of your topics, begin to produce some of your paragraphs. You don't have to start at the beginning. (In fact, starting with a paragraph that especially interests you or that you feel particularly confident about can be a good way to go.)

What you should do at this stage

- Produce topic sentences that clarify the topic the paragraph will explore or the argument it will make.
- Consider providing a link in the topic sentence with the previous topic so that it is clear how the topics are related.
- Introduce details; these could take the form of claims supported by evidence, examples, debates and your own critiques and counterpoints.

Stage 5: Find and read academic sources and make notes

You are now perfectly placed to find and read academic sources. All the work you've done will have established many search terms you can use when searching your university library databases or Google Scholar. These terms will also function as excellent 'filters' or 'spotlights' when you read the sources you find. We'll spend longer explaining what you should do at this stage because of its centrality to the process. The following chapters will build on this chapter by discussing many of the ways that others' work can feature in your assignments and the advanced skill of synthesis.

What you should do at this stage

Continue to search for topics or explore individual topics in more detail

You have two options at this point: you can continue your work in Stage 2 and search for new topics. However, if you think you have enough topics, then you can begin to systematically explore each of your topics (realistically, you'll probably do both).

- To continue a broad search for topics, use search terms from the question or similar broad terms when you search your library.

catalogue or Google Scholar. When reading articles and books, simply keep in mind your desire to expand your range of topics.

- If you want to focus on specific topics, then your search terms should be the topics themselves as well as keywords within them. You'll use these terms not just in library database searches but to find relevant material within sources themselves (see the next section). Within a topic, search for facts, similar and contrasting perspectives, interesting arguments, examples, useful concepts and theories, and so on. (See Chapter 10 for more details on what you can do with sources in your paragraphs.)

Use the following techniques to find relevant information within sources

a) Begin by assessing the title for relevance. If the title is relevant, move on to (b).

b) Read the article abstract (or overview of the book if available). If this material is relevant, move on to (c).

c) Either (1) Use 'Ctrl + F' (for PCs) or 'Cmd + F' (for Macs) to find when a source uses a term - read around the term and see whether the information is useful or (2) Read the introduction and conclusion of the article (or parts of the introduction and conclusion if a book). Focus on the 'bumps' (see Chapter 7): the subject and problem being addressed, the solution and so on. If you intend to write only a few words (say 10 to 20) about the source, as is often the case, then reading the introduction and conclusion may well give you enough material to use in your assignment. Make a note of the relevant material and why it's relevant (see Chapter 6) or even incorporate the material directly into a paragraph. If you haven't yet found what you are looking for in the source, then you may need to 'scan' it; move on to (d).

d) As we've mentioned, the topics and terms you have in mind when you read act like 'filters' or 'spotlights' that capture or illuminate relevant information. Rather than reading a source slowly, 'scan' it quickly to see when relevant terms and topics are mentioned. Scanning can be like 'overviewing' in that you can quickly review headings and topic sentences; it can also involve quickly reading individual paragraphs. Of course, 'Ctrl + F' performs a similar function; however, at times, a source will talk about something relevant without using the terms you have in mind. Chapter 11 contains an extended activity that will help you to practice scanning for information in a source.

Stage 6: Refine your plan

Having surveyed a number of academic sources and assimilated a lot of new information, you will likely find that your original plan will need to be modified.

What you should do at this stage

- Either while you are reading your sources or after you've read several of them, look over your original plan and make changes. Consider the following changes:
  1. Add topics to your discussion.
  2. Separate topics that were previously grouped together. (Perhaps you were going to cover two points within a paragraph but you decide to dedicate a paragraph to each.)
  3. Group topics that were previously separated. (Perhaps you had planned to dedicate a separate paragraph to two topics but you realize the topics should be discussed together in one paragraph.)
  4. Populate your topics with new relevant sources.
  5. Reconsider the order of your topics, including the level of abstraction of each topic.
- You should also further refine your thesis.

Stage 7: Produce a solid draft

You are now well placed to write your assignment. Having moved through the first six stages, you'll hopefully find that writing is not nearly as difficult as it might have been in the past. This is because you'll have already put in place all the fundamental components of your assignment: you know what topics you want to discuss, you know how they relate to one another, you understand the complexities of each of your topics, you have many sources to support each of your discussions, and your own thoughts about your topics will be well developed.

What you should do at this stage

- Go and write your paragraphs! As we suggested above, start where you feel most confident; you don't have to start with your first body paragraph or your introduction. (In fact, it's often a good idea to wait until the end to write – or heavily refine – your introduction.)
- Use your paragraphs to present facts, explore the complexities of your topics and present your own informed opinions. (Again, see the synthesis example in Chapter 12.)

- Once you have produced a solid draft, set it aside for a day or two and then revise it. This is very important, as you need to look over your work with 'fresh eyes' to be able to identify how it should be improved.
- Get a friend to look over your work. They will spot things you are unable to see. This is you implementing your own peer-review process!

Stage 8: Read opportunistically to find additional sources

We now reach a stage that is rarely used by undergraduate students but that can be very pleasurable and extremely useful. The idea is that once you've produced a solid draft, you now have an exceptional 'filter' or 'spotlight': the draft itself. Armed with this, you can return a final time to finding academic sources. You'll find that you can add at least several sources to your assignment in a short time because you'll be able to quickly see how what you read relates to what you have written.

What you should do at this stage

- As with Stage 5, enter keywords from the question and your specific topics into your library search engine or Google Scholar and find additional sources. You can also return to sources which you have already found but which didn't initially prove useful.
- Scan the sources for anything that could be relevant to any of your discussions. This could be additional evidence for a claim, a useful example or a counter-perspective that you could address.

Stage 9: Revise before submission

This stage is a continuation of Stage 7.

What you should do at this stage

- Depending on how much time you have, continue to revise your assignment, taking substantial breaks in between (at least several hours).
- Complete your introduction and conclusion in accordance with the conventions in your field. Ensure that there is a close fit between your introduction and conclusion and the content in the body of the assignment.
- Finalize your reference list, making sure that you have followed the requirements of your assignment in terms of formatting.
- Submit your assignment!

An extended example illustrating the early stages of the assignment-production process

We'll briefly illustrate two of the early stages of the assignment-production process: identifying topics and planning. The process through which an individual paragraph is developed is illustrated in Chapter 12. We are responding to the question 'Why do we laugh?' At the time of writing, I (Jamie) teach a course about comedy, humour and laughter (Cait helped design it). We'll be imagining that we are a student in this course.

Stage 1: Begin to establish topics for discussion: draw on what you've learned from class and set readings and what you already know

Below, we list a number of points that arose in the course that respond to the question, 'Why do we laugh?' Similar points can be found through a Google search. At this stage, we just present the points; we aren't looking for commonalities, nor are we thinking about the best order to discuss them.

1. There are the frequently encountered theories of comedy/humour. These are simplified, general theories that aim to explain many instances of comedy/humour:

   - We laugh when something *incongruous* or unexpected occurs.
   - We laugh when we feel *superior* to someone who has done something foolish.
   - We laugh to *release tension*.
   - We laugh when we *identify* with something, such as when a cat does something human.

2. Laughter is a social phenomenon: we laugh with other people much more than on our own.
3. Some argue that laughter evolved to help groups bond. Others say that it evolved to communicate to the group that a perceived threat wasn't a threat (for example, a perceived snake turned out to be a stick). An important point is that regardless of why laughter evolved, it has been adapted for many functions by different societies.
4. Socially, laughter is sometimes spontaneous or unintentional; sometimes it is intentionally added to conversation.
5. There is a 'primary frame' within which activities that relate to survival (such as work) occur. There is a 'secondary frame' within which play occurs. Laughter belongs in the secondary frame.
6. Laughter plays an important role in mate selection.

7. In politics, we laugh at 'enemy' politicians to make them less legitimate. Also, politicians use humour to attack their enemies. Some countries allow political satire; others do not.

8. Different cultures use humour in different ways. Consider Japanese game shows that generate humour from humiliating people. Consider the allegedly different approaches to humour by the English and the Americans. Consider the phenomenon or sacred clowning where social norms are permissibly subverted.

9. Some people seem to be allowed to be funny, such as men and bosses, whereas others, such as women and employees, are often not allowed.

10. We like to laugh at death.

11. It is admirable if we laugh at ourselves.

Stage 3: Plan: transform your topics into a provisional 'tree diagram' or 'skeleton' of your assignment

There are many ways to organize the above points. One way is to begin with a discussion of the evolutionary origins of laughter and then to explore a range of social functions that laughter now serves that are related to these origins. We present this in Figure 9.1. We aren't certain that the organization will work; perhaps there is too much overlap between some of the points (for instance, 1 and 2). But the plan certainly allows us to explore many of the points we identified, and we are well set to find academic sources that will help us make each of our points.

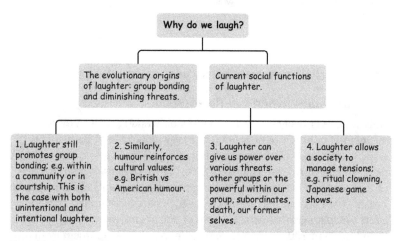

Figure 9.1   A provision tree diagram of our response to the question, 'Why do we laugh?'

Chapter 12 illustrates how to produce a paragraph about the evolution-ary origins of laughter.

ACTIVITY 9.2

The early stages of the research process: identifying topics and crafting a skeleton

We now give you the opportunity to practice the early stages in the assignment-production process. Below are three frequently encountered questions. Pick one and move through the first three stages of the research process:

1. Write down all the topics you think you should consider so as to provide a thorough exploration of the problem.

2. Do some Googling for general articles and perhaps search Google Scholar and your university library website for abstracts to learn about topics you haven't thought of.

3. Create a skeleton or tree diagram that will allow you to explore all the relevant topics in a systematic manner.

Task questions

- Is social media good or bad?
- Are genetically modified crops good or bad?
- Are we responsible for the welfare of others?

Some additional questions you might have

How do I know when I'm finished?

Nothing is ever really finished. You just stop working on it. A more meaningful question is: how good does my work have to be before I stop? A useful way of answering this question is by referring to the law of diminishing returns (see Figure 9.2). The law of diminishing returns tells us that, early on in a process, working hard (adding units of labour) yields sizeable benefits (output). However, as the process continues, additional effort yields smaller benefits. In terms of an assignment, let's consider a scale from 0 to 100. You will, say, be able to get an assignment from 0 to 50 (a pass) in 6 hours. Another 6 hours work will push the assignment to

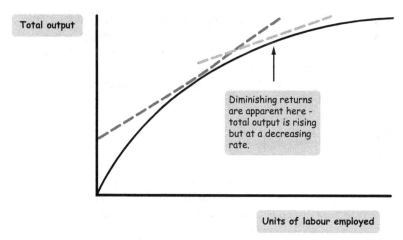

Total output

Diminishing returns
are apparent here -
total output is rising
but at a decreasing
rate.

Units of labour employed

Figure 9.2   The law of diminishing returns

65. Another 6 hours will get it to 75, and so on. As your studies continue, you'll get a sense of how much work is needed for you to achieve a mark you are satisfied with. In practical terms, we advise you to edit your work at least once and preferably three or four times. However, seven or eight edits might not be worth your while.

How many sources should I include in an assignment (or: when do I stop reading)?

Students often want to know how many sources to include in an assignment. There is no easy answer to this question; however, the following might be useful.

- You can always read more, but remember, it's not all about the number of sources. The main thing is to ensure that you cover the significant topics, show an awareness of key debates and make sure your own critical voice is present.
- Sometimes, assignment guidelines specify the minimum number of sources you should include. If so, going over this number by at least two or three looks good. So, if the minimum source requirement is 8, include 10 or 11.
- For short assignments (between 1,000 and 2,000 words), including 10 to 20 academic sources is usually reasonable.

- For dissertations, the number of sources should increase significantly, especially if the dissertation contains a literature review (which is common). Longer pieces of writing (50,000–100,000 words) often include 200 or more sources.
- Remember that it's not difficult to add several sources late in the assignment-production process by doing some last-minute opportunistic reading.

Conclusion

In this chapter, we've introduced the research process in relation to assignments such as essays and literature reviews – assignments that usually require you to include a range of sources. Our main advice is: don't begin the assignment-production process by reading lengthy academic sources, nor should you begin by trying to write the assignment. Rather, work your way slowly towards these activities first by working out what you already know and then reading widely to establish the topics you want to discuss in your assignment. Having done some planning and perhaps even some preliminary writing, you are well set to start reading academic sources. Search for information by reading for the 'bumps' (read introductions, headings and topic sentences), scanning and using computer assistance. Then when you are feeling confident, start producing your paragraphs. Consider doing some 'opportunistic reading' once you have a solid draft and make sure you edit your work two or three times.

Reading Critically (Part 1): Different Ways of Using Information in Your Writing, Including Critiquing

Introduction

In the previous chapter, we talked about how you can read to find topics to discuss in your assignments, but we didn't say much about what you can do in your paragraphs with the information you find. This brief chapter will introduce you to a number of things you can do, which will give you an excellent idea of what you should be looking for when you read. We call this chapter 'reading critically' because it encourages you, when you read, not to be a passive receiver of information but to think about the many functions information can serve in your own writing.

Remember that, at university, we are in the business of creating knowledge, which usually takes the form of solving problems. So, what you take from your sources should contribute in various ways to whatever solution you are working on. You could be establishing the significance of your subject, exploring the complexities within a topic, supporting a claim you'd like to make strengthening your position by pointing out the flaws in another's argument or combining information in an original way. (Chapter 12 will explore comparative reading, including synthesis, in more detail.) We'll conclude the chapter by discussing making evaluations or critiques.

Using information in your assignments

Box 10.1 outlines a range of ways that others' work can feature in your writing and provides examples of each. We've grouped the functions under four headings:

- speaking generally
- doing useful things with individual sources
- evaluating (critiquing)
- comparing, contrasting and synthesizing.

Many more functions and examples could be provided but this will get you thinking in the right direction! Once again, when you are aware of these functions, your reading will be much more focused and critical because you'll have a sense of all the ways that information from your sources can feature in your writing.

Box 10.1   Some ways of using information you find in your sources

The function of the information in your work	Examples of what you might write
Speaking generally (see also Chapter 13)	
Providing a history of scholarship	– X was first studied systematically in the early twentieth century (see, for example, Brown 1922). It received renewed interest in the 1950s (see Sokolov 1961).
Establishing the significance of your subject	– X has received significant attention in recent years. Major studies have been produced by Wong (2017) and Smith (2018). – As Saleh (2019) points out, X is important because…
Speaking generally about previous research	– Recent research has focused on X (for example, Wong 2017; Smith 2018; Saleh 2019).
Identifying significant research	– Wong's (2017) study has had considerable influence on the field.
Identifying a knowledge gap in research	– Many researchers have explored X (see, for example, Wong 2017; Smith 2018; Saleh 2019); however, the question of Y is yet to receive attention.

Presenting useful general information (for example, if you are establishing the context of a discussion)	– There are three broad perspectives about X. The first (see Smith 2018) is ...
Doing useful things with individual sources	
Making a claim or presenting a fact	– X has several health benefits (Wong 2017). – As Smith (2018) has demonstrated, there is a causal relationship between X and Y. – Saleh (2019) found that ... This is useful because ...
Providing an example	– X is, arguably, not suitable for children. For example, Smith (2018) describes how ...
Introducing a concept (the second example concerns a debated concept)	– This phenomenon can be understood to be an example of X. As Wong (2017) explains, X is ... – The concept of X is frequently encountered; however, there is still some disagreement about how best to define it. Saleh (2019) defines X as ... Smith (2018), on the other hand, defines it as ...
Presenting a method	– Saleh (2019) used method X to determine whether Y causes Z.
Explaining something	– Wong (2017) argued that ... Perhaps, she took this position because ...
Analysing (breaking something into parts, often to assist evaluation)	– Wong's (2017) argument has three components. First, ... Second, ... Third, ...
Adding to a perspective or approach	– In relation to X, Saleh (2019) argues that ... To this, we can add ...
Making evaluations (critiques)	
Identifying an omission in research	– Although Smith (2018) provides an excellent account of ..., he fails to consider ...
Identifying an error in research	– Saleh (2019) argues that ... However, it is illogical for her to suggest that ...

Making a positive evaluation	– Smith's (2018) exploration of X is notable for two reasons. First, …
Making an evaluation and suggesting an improvement	– Wong's (2017) approach is limited because … However, if we did X, the approach would be more useful.
Developing your position or approach by demonstrating a flaw in another's argument or approach	– Although Smith (2018) proposes X, if this were implemented in the context of Y, then there would be serious consequences. Thus, a better approach would be …
Comparing, contrasting and synthesizing	
Pointing out similarities	– Both Wong (2017) and Saleh (2019) identified …
Summarizing and grouping	– There have been two approaches to solving X. The first (see Smith 2018, Wong 2017 and Saleh 2019) addresses the problem from a mental-health perspective. The second …
Identifying a debate	– Researchers continue to debate the utility of X. On the one hand, Wong (2017) argues that …; on the other hand, Saleh (2019) suggests that …
Identifying conflicting findings	– Wong (2017) reports that …; however, Saleh (2019) found no evidence of …
Discussing what one writer says about another writer	– Smith's (2018) critique of Wong (2017) was insightful. He pointed out that …
Supporting a claim after contrasting different perspectives	– X has been debated in recent years. On the one hand, researchers such as Wong (2017) argue that … On the other hand, Saleh (2019) proposes that … Although Wong is correct in stating that …, ultimately Saleh's position is most credible because … Thus, the best approach is …
Developing your position or approach by combining components from different perspectives (this is 'synthesis' – see Chapter 12)	– None of the existing methods is suited to the current conditions. However, if we combine X from Smith's (2018) study with Y from Wong's (2017) study, then the outcome will be improved.

A few more words about making evaluations or critiques

As is hopefully becoming clear to you, once you've found information that is potentially relevant for your assignment, you should think about whether you agree with what's stated. In doing this, you'll be 'evaluating' or 'critiquing' the source. (These words are often used interchangeably; however, we'll use 'evaluating' because it's more neutral.) Evaluating doesn't mean that you should be able to find flaws in everything you read. Rather, it means scrutinizing the evidence and reasoning that are presented to support a claim and considering whether you find it convincing. Sometimes, especially when you are scrutinizing empirical work, you might find it difficult to make a clear assessment and you might conclude that the work seems reasonable as far as you are able to determine. This is fine. The main thing is that you are developing your critical thinking skills. The longer you spend in your field or discipline, the better you'll become at evaluating work.

Evaluating a source also involves thinking about how the information relates to *your* existing ideas about a topic. When reading, consider the following three questions:

- Does the information *confirm* my existing ideas?
- Does the information *expand* upon what I already know? That is, does the source deepen my understanding of a problem by introducing new topics, arguments or perhaps methods I should consider?
- Does the information *challenge* my existing ideas? If so, who is correct? Do I need to change my point of view, or can I demonstrate that what I read is incorrect?

Read with a mindset of 'receptive scepticism': be open to the information you are presented with but don't accept it without first assessing it.

Specific things to evaluate in a source

Box 10.1 gave you some ideas about what you can evaluate in a source. Box 10.2 provides a more substantial list. Some of the items are general, others are specific. Some relate to empirical work, others to argumentative (essayistic) work and some to both.

Box 10.2   Questions that can guide your evaluations

- Is the subject of the work worthy of our attention?
- Is the problem being addressed worthy of our attention?
- Is the method used to solve the problem appropriate?
- If the work is empirical, are the data reliable – will the same data be obtained in a replication?
- If the work is empirical, is a test valid – does it measure what it claims to measure?
- If the work is empirical, have statistics been appropriately analysed?
- If the work is empirical, have sample sizes been appropriate?
- Are claims supported by sufficient evidence and reasoning?
- Have all significant perspectives been considered?
- Has the analysis gone into sufficient detail?
- If a theory is used (a theory is an account of how the world works), does it adequately explain a phenomenon; conversely, is it a reasonable generalization from phenomena that have been observed?
- Is the work well structured and clearly expressed?
- Does the author have a conflict of interest?

But what is 'analysis'?

We often use the word 'analysis' in the context of critical thinking. The word might seem vague, but, really, what it describes is straightforward. Analysis involves breaking something into parts and then doing something with these parts: perhaps clarifying what's meant, drawing out the implications, comparing, contrasting or evaluating. We undertake analysis all the time. The trick will be for you to transfer your everyday analytical skills to the university context.

ACTIVITY 10.1

Everyday analysis

Evaluating is something we do every day. For example, many of us, having watched a movie, will then evaluate it. The first step is to work out which aspect of the movie we want to assess: the plot, the acting, the sets, the score and so on. If we choose 'acting', we could compare the performances and evaluate which was best. Having watched *The Last Jedi*, we might conclude, 'Daisy Ridley was compelling, but Carrie Fisher was wooden'. We would then present evidence to support our evaluation. We might also compare performances across different films. For example, 'Carrie Fisher was much more impressive in the original Star Wars movies'. To improve your critical thinking skills, get into the habit of making evaluations in your everyday life – or be more conscious of when you do make evaluations. You can start with movies or YouTube videos but you should also attempt to analyse news reports, political speeches and so on.

Your tasks

On your own or with a group:

- Watch a movie, pick an aspect of the movie to evaluate (critique) and then make your evaluation.
- Read or listen to a political speech. Evaluate individual claims and compare these claims with claims made by other politicians and also by the same politician in other contexts. How are the claims similar or different? Which claims do you prefer and why?

But I don't have any opinions!

Some students find it hard to be critical readers and writers; they understand that it's important, but they can't make it work. There is a simple solution to this problem (however, it's not always easy to implement). You need to be interested in your studies and immerse yourself in your courses. So, pick a degree that matters to you and go to class, pay attention, do parts of your set readings and start your assignments early. See yourself as being a member of your field of study, not merely an observer. And be patient.

Conclusion

The uncritical student will come across information in sources and mindlessly transfer it into their own work. Such a student isn't doing anything with the information. The critical student will always be thinking about what they can do with the information they read. They will also read with an attitude of 'receptive scepticism': they will be open to what they are reading and at the same time they will always be asking whether the claims made in a source are sufficiently supported by the evidence and reasoning presented. And this will be made possible because the student is interested in what they are studying.

An Extended Activity About How to Find, Evaluate and Use Information from a Single Source

Introduction

This chapter provides an extended activity that will demonstrate some of what we've been discussing in the previous chapters. The activity involves searching for information in an article that can help you answer a given question and beginning to think about how you might use this information. The article, 'Three Ways to Accelerate Science', is by Cori Bargmann (2018), a prominent neurobiologist. It's quite long – 1,500 words – but we've selected it to provide you with a realistic experience of searching ('scanning') for relevant information.

Activity instructions

Begin by becoming familiar with the article. The following 'overview' questions from Chapter 7 will guide you:

- What problem is being addressed?
- Why is the problem significant?
- What is the solution?
- What is the structure of the article (identify sections and read topic sentences)?

Once you have a sense of what the article's about, it's time to practise reading with specific questions (or 'filters' or 'spotlights') in mind. Do the following:

1. Select one of the focus questions below. Brainstorm the topic by thinking about (and writing down) why the question is significant and come up with some tentative responses to the question. The longer you spend doing this, the easier it will be to find relevant material in the article.
2. Scan the article with the question and your tentative responses in mind. Find the relevant information. Don't expect the article to provide a definitive answer to the question; this is unlikely given that the article is concerned with a different problem.
3. Consider how you might use the relevant information in the article as part of an answer to the question you selected. (Look back over the information in the previous chapter for some ideas about the different ways you can use information in your work.)

Focus questions:

- Is specialization beneficial?
- What are some problems with the normal avenues of academic publishing? How could academic publishing be improved?
- Which is superior, youth or age?

We provide a response to the 'overview' questions and the first focus question after the article. Responses to the second and third focus questions can be found at the back of the book.

The article: 'Three ways to accelerate science' by Cori Bargmann

Introduction

In 1987, I joined the lab of Robert Horvitz at the Massachusetts Institute of Technology in Cambridge as a postdoctoral fellow. I was fascinated by the idea of using genetics to probe the neural basis of behaviour. And a unique resource drew me to the tiny transparent worm *Caenorhabditis elegans*: a wiring diagram of the 302 neurons in the adult worm's nervous system.

Work led by John White, then a *C. elegans* researcher at the Medical Research Council's Laboratory of Molecular Biology (LMB) in Cambridge, UK, had mapped all the connections between the worm's neurons by slicing the animal into thousands of sections and tracing each cell using electron microscopy. This wiring diagram, combined with the worm's short life cycle of a few days, offered a tremendous opportunity to relate the development and function of the nervous system to genes and neurons. And it was just one of the many shared resources available for *C. elegans* research.

The findings made using *C. elegans* have been remarkable. Among these are the caspase system that controls programmed cell death; the netrin system that guides neuronal connectivity; and the post-transcriptional gene-regulatory pathways involving microRNAs and small interfering RNAs.

I believe that the success of these projects emerged in part from a unique research culture and infrastructure. Now I want to help put in place similar opportunities on a larger scale, as president of the Chan Zuckerberg Science Initiative, a philanthropic effort launched in late 2016 to support biomedical research.

Part 1: The three ingredients

What made the *C. elegans* field successful?

A common reference. By the mid-1960s, fruit flies and yeast had already been studied for decades. But biologist Sydney Brenner, then at the LMB, wanted to develop a new model organism for studying the big questions in development and neuroscience. He picked *C. elegans*.

The LMB group began realizing Brenner's goal by developing a shared infrastructure. Brenner and his PhD student Jonathan Hodgkin created genetic tools, such as strains of worms with well-characterized mutations, and mapped the functions of hundreds of genes. Biologist John Sulston led a team that described the complete lineage of all cells, documenting every step in the transformation of a single-cell embryo to the adult worm (J. E. Sulston *et al. Dev. Biol.* 100, 64–119; 1983). White, Brenner and their team mapped the connections of all of the worm's neurons, naming every neuronal cell and mapping its lineage and place in the circuit.

Descriptive science – observing, recording, describing and classifying phenomena – is often valued less than hypothesis testing. But the common resources that result help everyone. Every experiment I have done has been grounded in White and colleagues' wiring paper, affectionately known as *The Mind of a Worm* (J. G. White *et al. Phil. Trans. R. Soc. Lond. B* 314, 1–340; 1986).

The success of these projects, and the recognition of their value by the community, meant that it was easy to convince *C. elegans* researchers of the worth of the first genome projects discussed in the 1990s. They were similarly game for making and sharing the first RNAi libraries (collections of small interfering RNAs for disrupting gene function, matched to every gene in the worm's genome), the Wormbase organismal database (a repository of everything that's known about *C. elegans* biology) and, more recently, the global genetic-diversity resource CeNDR (www. elegansvariation.org).

Creative exploration. Today, people are often encouraged to stay in a research niche for long stretches of their careers – to learn 'more and more about less and less'. One effect of this is that students stay in the same fields as their advisers, and both learn less than they might have done had they diversified.

By contrast, the MRC mavens took a gamble that there were many interesting questions left in biology and that buying lots of lottery tickets – in the form of different research areas – would pay off for the success and prestige of the field. Thus, there was a conscious decision among those involved in the foundational work on *C. elegans* to maximize discovery by encouraging people to explore the worm's biology widely. When I joined his lab, Horvitz told me I could study any problem that could be addressed in a worm.

Openness. Today, two concerns tend to come up in discussions about releasing findings before their formal publication: is the work accurate, and will people steal the results?

When I started working on *C. elegans*, people published in a semiregular newsletter called the *Worm Breeder's Gazette* (*WBG*). Most of the groups that were using the worm as a model organism published in every issue; the one-page abstracts typically described a single result. The *WBG* was fast. A few weeks or months after you had a result, it would be out there for everyone to see. In fact, some *WBG* abstracts preceded papers by five years or more.

Some of the findings reported in the *WBG* didn't hold up long-term. And that was okay; results that can't be replicated soon get ignored. As for stealing others' work, I think that the very openness of the *C. elegans* field acted as a deterrent. Everyone knew what was in the *WBG*, and there was a clear expectation that if you used someone else's result, you included that person in your study or cited them. The scientists who read the *WBG* were the same ones who were going to review your grants, papers and case for promotion, so the implicit requirement to respect that culture had teeth. In many cases, the openness seemed to relieve tensions; people could find out in advance whether similar work was in progress in another lab and coordinate publications.

Part 2: Shaping science today

The mission of the Chan Zuckerberg Science Initiative, founded in 2016 by Mark Zuckerberg and Priscilla Chan, is to support science and technology that will make it possible to cure, prevent or manage all diseases by the end of the century. It's a bold goal. But the end of the century is still 82 years away. Going back in time a similar distance, much of modern medicine would have been unthinkable – from organ transplants and deep brain stimulation to treating cancer by manipulating the immune system.

All of these advances were built on a foundation of basic biomedical science. To enable the next generation of discoveries, we at the Chan Zuckerberg Initiative want all of biomedical science to be faster, more robust, sharable and scalable. We're starting a number of different programmes – both locally and globally – to try out ideas for accelerating science and driving collaboration.

First, we want to support scientific infrastructure projects that change the landscape for research fields. In collaboration with other groups and funders, we are supporting the Human Cell Atlas (HCA), an endeavour to map all the cells in the human body. For the trillions of cells that make up the human body, we don't know how many cell types there are, nor their exact numbers, locations, molecular compositions and spatial relationships in tissues and organs. Such knowledge could benefit all biologists who study humans.

In addition to funding experimental scientists working on the HCA, the Chan Zuckerberg Initiative is funding external collaborators and an in-house group of software engineers and computational biologists focused on developing new data platforms and tools for biomedical science. This is an opportunity, because many of the advances in technology that have happened in the commercial sector have not been available to academic science. As a neuroscientist, I take this personally: numerous recent innovations in machine learning and neural networks originated in neuroscience, so biologists should be able to share the benefits.

Second, to foster creativity, we plan to support people who want to work in new areas – especially young researchers setting up their own labs. Most scientists do their most creative work at this early stage of their careers. But – understandably – it's often hard to obtain funding unless you can demonstrate expertise in a particular area. The Chan Zuckerberg Initiative could fill a niche by taking on more risks than other funders. That risk is worthwhile if it brings people into biomedical areas in which the need is great but current research is narrowly directed. Unfortunately, disease-relevant fields can be some of the hardest to break into for someone with a new idea or approach. Certain disease foundations, such as the Hereditary Disease Foundation for Huntington's disease or the Simons Foundation Autism Research Initiative, have done this well in the past. But we think that there is room to scale up this model to many other biomedical problems.

Finally, on openness. We believe that research advances when people build on each other's work. So our principles include making data, protocols, reagents and code freely available for other scientists to use. As an example of this approach, the HCA has committed to making its reference data publicly available after quality-control checks. Indeed, the Chan Zuckerberg Initiative engineering team and our HCA collaborators are building all of the software for the 'data coordination' arm of the project on the open-source platform Github.

We're also supporting external groups that share these values and goals. For instance, we're funding bioRxiv, the largest and fastest-growing preprint repository for the biological sciences – and a leader in bringing biology towards the level of sharing that's expected in the physical and computer sciences.

The Chan Zuckerberg Initiative is just starting, and we have a lot to learn. But I've been lucky to work in areas in which the free exchange of ideas and results is the norm. In my experience, such an approach creates the most dynamic fields. Now I have the chance to lead a new funding venture and to explore whether openness or dynamism comes first. After all, as scientists we do experiments; as funders, we can do experiments too.

Our responses to the questions

The overview of the article

What problem is being addressed by the article?

More broadly, Bargmann identifies the mission of the Chan Zuckerberg Science Initiative as being 'to cure, prevent or manage all diseases by the end of the century'. However, the specific problem addressed by the article is the one implied in the title: how can we accelerate scientific research?

Why is the problem significant?

The article doesn't explicitly address significance, but we can figure it out. The broad problem is significant because disease is a major source of misery for humanity. The specific problem is significant because scientific research is hard. It's not enough to put scientists in a lab. They usually need to be part of a broader institution whose philosophy and accompanying practices are conducive to good science.

What is the solution?

The solution, in short, is that the Chan Zuckerberg Science Initiative will employ the research philosophy that allowed research in the *C. elegans* field to be so successful; namely, ensuring that research occurs within innovative programmes, supporting young researchers who want to work in new areas and making various aspects of the foundation's research freely available.

What is the structure of the article?

The article begins with an introduction that provides some background on the research conducted in the lab of Robert Horvitz in relation to the *C. elegans* worm. The introduction culminates by articulating Bargmann's broader aim: to reproduce the research culture that was so successful in Horvitz's lab in the Chan Zuckerberg Science Initiative. The body of the article is in two parts. In the first part, the three successful aspects of the research culture in Horvitz's lab are presented. The second part explains how these aspects will be adopted by Chan Zuckerberg Science. Hopefully, you see how the argument is manifested in the article's structure – this highlights the value in reading to identify structure.

The focus question: Is specialization beneficial?

What is the significance of the question and what are your tentative responses?

The question 'Is specialization beneficial?' is regularly encountered in discussions about the tertiary education system and research and training more generally. There are clear benefits for individuals, organizations and so on, from focusing on a narrow subject for a long time; namely, they gain mastery that helps them solve challenging problems within the subject. However, there are also drawbacks. Perhaps specialization leads to information or techniques from beyond the narrow subject being ignored, and perhaps because of this, specialists become set in their ways. There is much more that could be said about this!

Which aspects of the article are relevant?

Interestingly, Bargmann doesn't use the word 'specialization', so this is a case of scanning not just for a term (or using 'Ctrl + F') but for an idea. Under the heading 'Creative exploration', she speaks of people being 'encouraged to stay in a research niche for long stretches of their careers' (that is, learning 'more and more about less and less'). This is a common way of defining specialization. She goes on to clarify that the kind of specialization she is talking about is students 'staying in the same fields as their advisers'. She argues that, if this happens, 'both learn less than they might have done had they diversified'. She is in favour of encouraging young researchers to move into new areas, the idea being that this is like 'buying lots of lottery tickets'.

How could the information be used?

A logical way to respond to the question 'Is specialization beneficial?' would be first to explore the beneficial aspects of specialization and then the problematic aspects. Bargmann's remarks could be used to contribute to the second part, specifically to a discussion of 'intergenerational specialization' (we made up this term!). Using her remarks, we could argue that although it is unquestionably useful for individuals to focus on specific subjects and indeed problems for extended periods, it is beneficial for a field if individuals within it branch out in many directions rather than falling into the grooves created by the older generation. The precise point would be that, when individuals branch out, it is much more likely that bold new discoveries will be made (winning the lottery) and that often this is more desirable than making small additions to existing knowledge.

You can see that the point we make sticks closely to Bargmann's point but with an innovative flourish or two (for example, the concept 'intergenerational specialization'). Our overall response to the question would bring into dialogue a range of perspectives and ultimately produce a synthesis of these perspectives. Such a synthesis would be a statement such as this: 'Specialization is, for the most part, good. It has generated many benefits for society. However, it should at times be tempered. It is important for specialists to maintain broad interests and to mix with diverse fields so that different fields can benefit from one another's knowledge. Specialists should also consider branching out in new directions from time to time to avoid stagnating and to increase the possibility of bold new discoveries being made'.

12

Reading Critically (Part 2): Comparative Reading and Synthesis

Introduction

Given that much academic work involves not simply learning what individual sources say but exploring ideas spread across a field of study or discipline, you should always think about how sources relate to one another and about how you can combine the ideas from multiple sources in new ways. By doing this – by reading comparatively and synthesizing – you are becoming part of an academic discussion. And the more you practice, the more you'll become an expert in your field. In this chapter, we'll say a little more about comparative reading and synthesis before presenting an extended worked example.

Comparative reading: identifying similarities

Identifying similarities between sources is an important academic skill. As we've mentioned, within any academic field, relevant information is dispersed across thousands of sources. A consequence of this is that many sources are concerned with similar topics, make similar claims, use similar methods and so on. Amongst other things, if multiple sources are concerned with the same subject, then you can be confident that the subject is significant. Also, if you want to make a claim that's made by several sources or use a similar method, then you'll have considerable support for doing so: the choices you make in your research are much stronger if they are supported by two or three sources rather than just one. Finally, similar claims can complement one another by providing a more complete understanding of a phenomenon. You'll see this below in the example of synthesis.

Comparative reading: contrasting (and more evaluating)

Contrasting involves identifying differences between sources. These could be different interpretations of a phenomenon or data, different methods for solving a problem, different recommendations, world views and so on. By identifying differences between sources, you'll be exploring the complexities of your subject and helping to ensure that you are addressing all of the dimensions of whatever problem you are tackling. Doing these things will make your own solution all the more credible. Once you've identified a contrast, it's important to ask why the perspectives differ. And once you've determined this, you should determine which perspective you prefer – or perhaps you think that both perspectives are wrong and that you have a superior perspective!

Synthesizing

Synthesizing is a key skill not just in university but in life. It involves taking aspects of existing solutions and using them to solve new problems. This technique is used when writing essays or literature reviews or developing methods within empirical work. But we also use synthesis when building a house or writing a song. Much of what you produce at university will involve synthesis, and often the originality in a piece of work lies largely in its synthesis. This means that if you want to innovate (be original), not every aspect of your work has to be original. Often, the originality is a flourish built on a firm foundation of synthesis.

ACTIVITY 12.1

Identifying synthesis in everyday life

Think about a creative endeavour you like. It could be fashion, architecture, music, cooking or something else. Pick a specific thing, such as an outfit, a building, a song or a meal. Identify all the components that constitute it. Now think about where you've seen, heard or tasted the components before. Think about why this particular combination is successful (or not!). If we are talking about a nice pasta sauce, perhaps there's a pleasant interplay between the sweet tomato flavour (thanks to the vine-ripened cherry tomatoes and caramelized onions), the capers, the salt, the pepper and the coriander. You get the idea. Strong arguments or sound methods are no different. It's all about synthesis.

Box 12.1   Synthesizing information within a specific topic

1. Identify all the topics that are relevant to your subject or problem (see Box 9.1).

2. Select a topic.

3. Search for sources related to the topic using keywords, reference lists and so on.

4. Identify the positions of individual sources. (Try to limit yourself to reading abstracts, introductions and conclusions.)

5. Group similar positions (identify patterns).

6. Clarify the nature of the differences between positions.

7. Evaluate (critique) the various positions.

8. Combine or synthesize the various positions in your own solution. Add your own points of originality whenever possible.

But how exactly do you synthesize? In part, we've covered this question when discussing the research process in Chapter 9 (see Box 9.1). There, we explored synthesis across an entire assignment. The synthesis involved finding all the different topics you ought to discuss to ensure good coverage of your subject and problem. Box 12.1 explains how to synthesize in relation to a specific topic of discussion within an assignment.

Note that by 'positions' we mean arguments, methods and so on. What you focus on will vary from one assignment to another.

An extended worked example demonstrating synthesis

The steps to produce a good synthesis might seem a little abstract. So that you can get a good sense of how they work, we now provide an extended worked example. Let's again consider the question, 'Why do we laugh?' When developing this example, we limited ourselves to around two and a half hours on steps 3 to 7 to keep it realistic. (If we were producing an academic article, we'd have spent much more time searching.) If you are inexperienced, you'll likely need more time. But the point is that it would have taken us 20 or more hours if we had read every word of every source we found.

1. Identify all the topics that are relevant to your subject or problem

As we noted in Chapter 9, the question 'Why do we laugh?' can be approached from many angles. (Look back over the example in Chapter 9 for the details.) Here is our summary:

- There has been a lot written about 'humour theories' (that is, the dynamics of jokes and other humorous events).
- Overlapping with this is the broader discussion of the many ways in which laughter functions in different societies. This ranges from the question of why we like laughing together in movie theatres, to how we use laughter to manage conversations, to how laughter functions in politics.
- A very useful topic is the evolutionary function of laughter. The idea is that laughter evolved to serve a specific purpose but this purpose has been adapted (or 'co-opted') for many additional purposes.

2. Select a topic

A manageable topic for this example is the evolutionary function of laughter.

3. Search for sources related to the topic

Using our university library search engine, we entered combinations of the following search terms into the 'title' category (we also could have entered the terms into a 'subject' category which would have provided a greater range of results): 'evolution', 'evolutionary', 'laughter', 'humour'. We found around 20 articles with relevant titles (we didn't search for books). We would have found more sources if we had added more search terms, included books, explored the reference lists of the 20 articles and so on.

4. Identify the positions of individual sources

We largely read abstracts, introductions and conclusions. In one or two cases, we scanned relevant sections, namely the sections that clearly talked about the evolutionary reasons for laughter. Of the 20 articles, some were too specific or inaccessible to be useful. We ended up finding useful information in 11 of the articles. Box 12.2 contains the most useful quotations we found in each article.

Box 12.2   The most useful quotations regarding the evolutionary function of laughter

A. 'Spontaneous laughter evolved as an honest signal of cooperative intent' (Bryant and Aktipis, 2014).

B. 'Laughter plays an important role in social bonding. In particular, it allows for larger social groups to be maintained' (Dezecache and Dunbar, 2012).

C. 'Laughter is used to influence the affective state of listeners' (Owren and Bachorowski, 2003).

D. 'Laughter evolved to communicate to the group that a perceived threat is not a threat' (Ramachandran, 1998).

E. 'Humor develops from aggression in males and is evolutionarily related to sexual selection' (Shuster, 2012).

F. 'Shared appreciation of humor provides a particularly effective means of identifying others with the relevant preferences and knowledge' (Curry and Dunbar, 2013).

G. 'Laughter and humour evolved 2–4 million years ago and promoted resource-building and social play during the fleeting periods of safety and satiation that characterized early bipedal life. Laughter and humour have since been co-opted for various novel functions' (Gervais and Wilson, 2005).

H. 'Both sexes were more likely to initiate humor and to respond more positively and consider the other person to be funny when initially attracted to that person' (Li et al., 2009).

I. 'Humour either functions primarily for natural selection (i.e. humour benefits survival of the individual), group selection (i.e. humour benefits the social evolution of a group), or mate selection (i.e. humour provides reproductive significance for male–female interactions)' (Eisend, 2018).

J. 'Laughter was an early consequence of bipedalism and can be studied to help us understand the evolution of speech' (Provine, 2017).

K. 'Infant humans and great apes share similar tickle-induced vocalisations' (Ross et al., 2009).

5. Group similar positions (identify patterns)

Some of the sources can be easily grouped, whereas others are outliers. Note that after we grouped the sources, it wasn't always obvious to us what we'd do with the information. The grouping helped to clarify our thoughts. Also, some of the sources can be included in multiple groups.

Group bonding

The most obvious grouping is the idea that laughter (and its close relative, 'humour') evolved to facilitate group bonding. Articles A, B, D, F, G and I each provide complementary perspectives on this. By 'complementary', we mean that each provides a slightly different angle on what seems to be the same phenomenon. See Box 12.3.

Box 12.3 The quotations that are concerned with group bonding

A) 'Spontaneous laughter evolved as an honest signal of cooperative intent' (Bryant and Aktipis, 2014).

B) 'Laughter plays an important role in social bonding. In particular, it allows for larger social groups to be maintained' (Dezecache and Dunbar, 2012).

D) 'Laughter evolved to communicate to the group that a perceived threat is not a threat' (Ramachandran 1998).

F) 'Shared appreciation of humor provides a particularly effective means of identifying others with the relevant preferences and knowledge' (Curry and Dunbar, 2013).

G) 'Laughter and humour evolved 2–4 million years ago and promoted resource-building and social play during the fleeting periods of safety and satiation that characterized early bipedal life. Laughter and humour have since been co-opted for various novel functions' (Gervais and Wilson, 2005).

I) 'Humour either functions primarily for natural selection (i.e. humour benefits survival of the individual), group selection (i.e. humour benefits the social evolution of a group), or mate selection (i.e. humour provides reproductive significance for male–female interactions)' (Eisend, 2018).

Laughter and mate selection

Articles E, H and I all mention a relationship between laughter and humour and mate selection. See Box 12.4.

Box 12.4   The quotations that are concerned with mate selection

E) 'Humour develops from aggression in males and is evolutionarily related to sexual selection' (Shuster, 2012).

H) 'Both sexes were more likely to initiate humor and to respond more positively and consider the other person to be funny when initially attracted to that person' (Li et al., 2009).

I) 'Humour either functions primarily for natural selection (i.e. humour benefits survival of the individual), group selection (i.e. humour benefits the social evolution of a group), or mate selection (i.e. humour provides reproductive significance for male–female interactions)' (Eisend, 2018).

Deeper evolutionary origins

It's hard to know what to do with articles J and K. They are not obviously useful for answering the question, 'Why do we laugh?' Nonetheless, they both say something about the more distant evolutionary origins of laughter. Perhaps article G could be added to this group as it mentions early bipedalism. Article D also seems to be 'evolutionarily prior' to the other articles in that it arguably identifies the earlier mechanism that was then adopted (or 'co-opted') for group bonding. See Box 12.5.

Box 12.5   The quotations that are concerned with deeper evolutionary origins

D) 'Laughter evolved to communicate to the group that a perceived threat is not a threat' (Ramachandran, 1998).

G) 'Laughter and humour evolved 2–4 million years ago and promoted resource-building and social play during the fleeting periods of safety and satiation that characterized early bipedal life. Laughter and humour have since been co-opted for various novel functions' (Gervais and Wilson, 2005).

J) 'Laughter was an early consequence of bipedalism and can be studied to help us understand the evolution of speech' (Provine, 2017).

K) 'Infant humans and great apes share similar tickle-induced vocalisations' (Ross et al., 2009).

Laughter and power

Perhaps articles C, D and E can be grouped together because they are broadly concerned with power. However, this grouping is tentative.

Box 12.6   The quotations that are concerned with power

C) 'Laughter is used to influence the affective state of listeners' (Owren and Bachorowski, 2003).

D) 'Laughter evolved to communicate to the group that a perceived threat is not a threat' (Ramachandran, 1998).

E) 'Humor develops from aggression in males and is evolutionarily related to sexual selection' (Shuster, 2012).

6. Clarify the nature of the differences between positions

Almost all of the claims are potentially complementary, meaning they are concerned with different aspects of the same phenomenon: bonding or cooperation. However, articles C and E stand out as having a contradictory perspective: they link laughter and humour with aggression and power.

7. Evaluate (critique) the various positions

Let's be honest: it's not that easy to critique most of the positions without having more information and indeed having expert knowledge of the subject. However, we can try to analyse the tension just mentioned by drawing on common knowledge. Specifically, although the image of people laughing *together* readily comes to mind, whether this be in a movie theatre or on the internet, we are also aware that laughter is related to superiority: we laugh when people hurt themselves. Thus, there seems to be at least some truth in the idea that the evolution of laughter is related not just to group bonding but to aggression or power.

8. Combine or synthesize the various positions in your own solution. Add your own points of originality whenever possible.

Below is a paragraph that synthesizes the above information in response to the question, 'Why do we laugh?' You'll note that to 'glue' the different perspectives together requires a fair amount of work. *This is where your own critical faculties are required*. The more you know about a topic, the easier it is to come up with this glue.

The synthesis

As we try to understand why we laugh, a logical place to begin is to explore the evolutionary origins of laughter. That there is an evolutionary origin for laughter can be supported in several ways. First, there is the obvious fact that laughter is ubiquitous across cultures. Second, studies have linked laughter with bipedalism (Provine, 2017) and have identified similarities between the tickle-induced vocalizations in infant humans and great apes (Ross et al., 2009). It is significant that infant humans laugh; this provides further support for the claim that laughter evolved rather than being a learned response. However, the evolutionary function of laughter remains difficult to pin down. Many researchers argue that laughter evolved to promote group cohesion (see Bryant and Aktipis, 2014; Dezecache and Dunbar, 2012; Curry and Dunbar, 2013; Gervais and Wilson, 2005; Eisend, 2018), the point being that the group that laughs together can better cooperate and be larger, both of which, we imagine, promoted the survival of the members within the group. Others align laughter and its close relative, humour, with mate selection (see Li et al., 2009; Shuster, 2012; Eisend, 2018). And notably, Shuster (2012) argues that humour evolved from aggression in males. Owren and Bachorowski (2003) also identify power as being part of the evolution of laughter. The functions of group bonding and mate selection are easily reconciled: we laugh in mate selection situations to indicate to the potential mate that we are willing to form a group with them. However, it is more challenging to reconcile the function of group bonding with the function of aggression, as the two seem to be in conflict. Perhaps a partial reconciliation is possible if we consider Ramachandran's (1998) argument that, prior to coming to promote group cohesion, laughter functioned to communicate to the group that a perceived threat is not a threat; for example, a snake turned out to be a stick. Perhaps we now laugh at potential threats to diminish their power over us; in this way, laughter can be linked

---

Left margin annotations:

This topic sentence introduces the focus of the paragraph: exploring the evolutionary origins of laughter. It also links the discussion with the broader purpose of the essay: understanding why we laugh.

We use this transitional sentence to mark our movement to the main point of the paragraph and to acknowledge that we are about to explore the complexities we uncovered in our reading.

Next, we group the sources that align laughter with mate selection.

The paragraph now moves from presenting the complexities of others' perspectives to analyzing these perspectives.

Right margin annotations:

We begin our synthesis by using articles J and K to make the preliminary argument that there is an evolutionary origin for laughter.

Here we group the similar perspectives about the bonding function of laughter.

This is a synthesis of all the perspectives just mentioned.

The third perspective about the evolutionary function of laughter is presented.

This concluding sentence summarizes what has been achieved in the paragraph and explains how this information will be used in the remainder of the essay.	with aggression. In short, there is strong evidence that laughter has an evolutionary origin and that this involved laughter functioning to strengthen group bonds while also diminishing threats to the group. As shall be argued, although laughter has been adapted for many purposes, these functions are present in almost all scenarios.

ACTIVITY 12.2

Produce your own synthesis

We now give you an opportunity to practice synthesis. In one paragraph, synthesize the below quotations in response to the question: 'Are there sex differences in intelligence?' As we've already found the quotations, you can begin with Step 5 from Box 12.1:

- Group similar positions (identify patterns).
- Clarify the nature of the differences between positions.
- Evaluate (critique) the various positions.
- Combine or synthesize the various positions in your own solution. Add your own points of originality whenever possible.

The following provides some context for the question. The issue of sex differences in intelligence continues to engage researchers and engender public debate. To clarify the question, when we are talking about 'sex differences', we are talking about variations between groups. Given that there is enormous variability within the groups themselves, even if there is, say, a small average difference between the sexes on some variable, this allows us to say very little about the attributes of individuals from either group. That is, you'll find women and men who excel in various measures of intelligence and women and men who do poorly on the same measures of intelligence. Also, this task is not focusing on the causes of differences, if they exist; one argument is that the causes of these differences are social rather than biological (see, for example, Fine, 2010). Finally, this task will be easier if you do some Googling. Consider looking up terms such as 'general intelligence' and see how they are defined and identify the debates surrounding them.

a) '[M]en and women have nearly identical IQs but […] men have a broader distribution. [T]he larger variation among men means that there are more men than women at either extreme of the IQ distribution' (Penrose, 1963).

b) '[S]ome data suggest a slight advantage for males [for general intelligence], and larger male TBV [total brain volume] is typically proposed as a potential explanation. On the other hand, most research indicates sex differences in general intelligence are negligible, and it has been hypothesized that the extra male brain volume might then be devoted to those specific skills in which males usually excel – mainly visuospatial abilities' (Burgaleta et al., 2012).

c) 'Males have a slight but consistently wider distribution than females at both ends of the range' (Deary et al., 2010).

d) 'Sex differences in problem solving have been systematically studied in adults in laboratory situations. On average, men perform better than women at certain spatial tasks…. They also outperform women in mathematical reasoning tests and in navigating their way through a route. Further, men exhibit more accuracy in tests of target-directed motor skills – that is, in guiding or intercepting projectiles. Women, on average, excel on tests that measure recall of words and on tests that challenge the person to find words that begin with a specific letter or fulfil some other constraint. They also tend to be better than men at rapidly identifying matching items and performing certain precision manual tasks, such as placing pegs in designated holes on a board' (Kimura, 2002).

e) 'The question of sex difference in intelligence has been debated from the early years of the twentieth century. The almost unanimous consensus has been that there is no sex difference in "general intelligence" […] There are, however, sex differences in a number of specific abilities' (Liu and Lynn, 2015).

f) '[G]ender differences in general intelligence are small and virtually non-existent' (Brody, 1992).

g) '[S]ex differences have not been found in general intelligence' (Halpern, 2000).

h) 'Overall, we agree with the conclusion of Burgaleta et al. (2012) and Escorial et al. (2015) that within subgroups or at the individual level, larger male brains do not necessarily have to be accompanied with higher general intelligence. Nevertheless, the present study also clearly indicates that, at the group level, there is a sex difference in g [general intelligence] and that differences in brain size likely play a relevant role in this' (van der Linden et al., 2017).

13

Reading to Understand Your Field

Introduction

Long before you begin your assignments and long after you finish them, you should be thinking about your field of study or discipline. This is for two closely related reasons. First, as mentioned in Chapter 2, to produce strong assignments, especially at higher levels, you should use your assignments to demonstrate your understanding of your field. Second, one of the main points of a university education is to make you an expert, at least to some extent, in your field. Once you are an expert in your field, you'll be able to meaningfully engage with much that happens within it: you'll be able to understand and evaluate what researchers are talking about and quickly assimilate new information and even devise and solve important problems. It's this versatility that will make you a strong researcher or, indeed, attractive to an employer. One way to think about your field is to think of it as having a 'shape'. This shape is made up of many dimensions, including the types of problems it tries to solve, the field's history and key debates. In this chapter, we'll discuss the concept of the 'field' in more detail before giving you the tools for understanding the shape of your field. Many of our examples are drawn from the introductions to articles. This is because it is in introductions that researchers tend to establish how their own work contributes to the existing field of knowledge.

What exactly is a 'field'?

Put simply, a 'field', which is also known as a 'discipline', is a branch of knowledge or area of study. Some fields are well established: they have a long history, a wide range of academic journals and conferences and are taught at almost all universities. Others are far less established: they have arisen only in recent decades, have fewer journals and conferences and are taught in a limited number of universities. Also, all fields overlap to varying degrees, and frequently fields have 'sub-fields' (or 'sub-disciplines'). Often, there is no consensus about the boundaries between fields or indeed where to locate sub-fields. Some academics conduct much of their work within a very specific field, whereas others move between fields or produce knowledge that crosses fields. Let's consider a couple of well-established fields: Chemistry and Political Science.

Chemistry is a field of study within the Natural Sciences. It has been practiced for centuries if not millennia, there are many academic journals and conferences dedicated to it, and it's taught at almost all universities. Chemistry is unquestionably a discrete field; however, it nonetheless overlaps with other fields, especially in the Natural Sciences, such as Physics and Biology, and the Applied Sciences, such as Engineering and Medicine. For example, if you were an astrochemist, you'd be interested in Chemistry in the broader context of the universe, and your work would overlap considerably with work done in Astronomy; indeed, you might call yourself a molecular astrophysicist!

Political Science is a field within the Social Sciences. Political Science, which is concerned with the decisions that are made in relation to groups of people or, more narrowly, with issues of governance, resource allocation and power, has been discussed for millennia. However, only in the last century or so has it established itself as a discrete academic field, after breaking away from Political Philosophy. Even more so than Chemistry, its various sub-fields overlap with other fields. For example, if you called yourself a Political Economist, you would be interested in the relationship between economics and governance and society. You would likely engage with the work of economists, historians, sociologists, anthropologists, philosophers and even statisticians, geographers and psychologists. At the same time, you might work in an Economics or Sociology department, not a Political Science department.

How can I begin to understand the 'shape' of my field?

No doubt, you are now thinking: 'OK, so what do I need to do to begin to understand the shape of my field?' First, the longer you are immersed in your field, the more you'll come to understand it. However, there are some basic questions you can keep in mind that will accelerate your understanding. These are presented in Box 13.1. We'll expand on the questions below and provide examples of when sources address these questions, so you can see how to read to find answers to them. All sources address these questions in some way, most commonly in introductions and literature reviews; introductory texts and Wikipedia address them explicitly.

Box 13.1   The questions you should ask to understand your field

1. What does the field study? (What types of problems is the field concerned with?)

2. What counts as knowledge in the field? (What is true according to the consensus within the field?)

3. What methods are used to create knowledge (solve problems) within the field?

4. What are the limitations of the knowledge base? (What makes developing knowledge challenging?)

5. What is the history of the field? (When did it begin? Did it grow out of other fields? What are its major achievements? Who are its important figures? How has it changed?)

6. What are the important debates within the field? Have these debates always been present, or are they new?

7. What are the key concepts and theories within the field? (These are often closely related to the problems and debates within the field.)

8. What other fields is the field related to? What is similar and different between the related fields? What critiques do the related fields make of one another?

9. What does the future hold for your field? (What problems will it explore?)

10. Where do you locate yourself within the field? Which aspects of your field most interest you? For example, are you attracted to a certain school of thought? What concerns do you have about your field?

Stop and think about your field

Much of the time at university, you'll be busy going to lectures and completing assignments. However, from time to time, you should stop and reflect on your field.

Your task: At the start of your university career (or now!) and every subsequent year, write down answers to the questions in Box 13.1. Be as honest as you can be: early on you may well answer, 'I have no idea' to some of the questions. You should also write down issues that you are trying to get to the bottom of; for example, 'I still don't really understand what is meant by X'. In time, your responses will become more refined as you continue to answer your own questions. Look back at your responses periodically to see how your understanding has grown. Your responses will provide a wonderful record of your intellectual development.

1. What does the field study? (What types of problems is the field concerned with?)

To understand your field, you need to understand what belongs within it; that is, you need to understand what phenomena – or things – it studies and what problems it tries to solve. Any one problem you are addressing will be much more meaningful if you understand how it relates to other problems. Also, you should understand how the field is structured with respect to the sub-fields within it.

To gain an overview of what your field studies, once again, reading introductory texts and Wikipedia pages is always useful. But you can also do things such as look over the titles of courses offered by universities and the corresponding course descriptions.

Consider Psychology. A glance at the Wikipedia entry tells us that Psychology is concerned with understanding behaviour and the mind and that, as a social science, it aims to understand individuals and groups by establishing general principles (patterns of thinking and behaviour) and by studying specific cases. We also learn that psychology is concerned largely with helping people. The remainder of the Wikipedia page details the specific areas of study, or 'sub-fields' within psychology as well as other aspects of the field such as its history and the methods it employs. We gain a complementary overview by noting the undergraduate Psychology courses offered by a university (UNSW

Sydney in Australia – where we work). We see the following sub-fields and their associated courses:

- Mental health issues: 'Abnormal Psychology', 'Psychology of Addiction' and 'Clinical perspectives on Anxiety Mood and Stress'
- Personality: 'Assessment Personality and Psychopathology'
- Perception: 'Perception and Cognition', 'Vision and the Brain'
- The functioning of the brain: 'Cognitive Science'
- How the individual relates to society: 'Social Psychology'
- How the individual develops: 'Developmental Psychology'
- Research methods and statistics: 'Research Methods 2', 'Research Methods 3', 'Multivariate Data Analysis'

You will hopefully already note the 'branching' nature of a field: one field branches into several sub-fields, each of which has further branches. You will learn about these branches by taking the courses themselves and by exploring sources.

In Example 13.1, we demonstrate how you can read to recognize both the different objects of study within a sub-field and the broader fields that this sub-field sits within. The sub-field is 'bullying in adolescence'. The example is drawn from the article, 'Multidisciplinary Approaches to Research on Bullying in Adolescence', from the special issue 'Innovative Approaches to Research on Adolescent Bullying: A Review of Multidisciplinary Research' in the journal *Adolescent Research Review*. Note that even before we read the article, we gain important information about how the field of Psychology is structured just by reading the titles of the journal, special issue and article. We depict this information in Figure 13.1. We see that 'bullying in adolescence' is one aspect of 'adolescence' that can be studied, just as 'adolescence' is one aspect of 'Developmental Psychology' and so on.

Figure 13.1   The branching nature of a field

Example 13.1   Identifying different objects of study in a sub-field (bullying in adolescence) and the broader fields within which the sub-field sits

This example is drawn from the introduction to the article 'Multidisciplinary approaches to research on bullying in adolescence' by Holt et al. (2016). We highlight all the places where the article says something about the objects of study within the sub-field of 'bullying in adolescence' and the broader fields within which 'bullying in adolescence' sits. Given that bullying in adolescence can be studied in many fields, this example is also relevant to Question 8 in Box 13.1.

From the beginning of the introduction

This tells us that bullying can be studied as a public health problem; that is, we can explore how bullying affects the population as a whole, not just individuals.

Bullying can also be studied within the field of law.

This tells us that bullying in adolescence is potentially a different problem from bullying in children.

Bullying remains a pressing public health problem in the United States. Increasingly, scholars have considered precursors, predictors, and consequences of bullying involvement as well as examined how to bolster the effectiveness of bullying prevention programs. Coupled with the research attention to bullying in the last few decades, there has been a significant expansion of states with laws mandating K-12 schools address bullying; whereas in 1999 only one state had enacted legislation (Georgia), as of 2015 all 50 states passed anti-bullying legislation. Despite these efforts from research and legal perspectives, there remain gaps in researchers' understanding of bullying. In particular, intervention research on bullying among adolescents, in contrast to children, remains limited. To date, research on bullying has been conducted primarily in the fields of psychology and education, but it is possible that other disciplines might offer novel and innovative approaches to understanding bullying and effective bullying interventions. As such, the purpose of this special issue is to suggest that one potentially fruitful approach to move research on adolescent bullying forward is to draw from disciplines that have been less central to, or to date not involved in, the discourse around bullying. In this introductory article, we first provide a brief overview of what is known about why bullying in adolescence should be a specific focus of research by describing: bullying rates

These are three topics that can be studied within the broader subject of bullying.

Prevention of bullying is another topic that is studied within the broader subject of bullying.

Bullying can be studied within psychology and education.

This does not say anything new, but it is useful in that it implies that by considering the 'precursors, predictors and consequences' of bullying, we are, in effect, trying to 'understand' bullying.

Specific problems that will help us 'understand' bullying are presented. ⟵

and correlates; the overlap between bullying and other victimization exposures that increase among adolescents; and what is known about the effectiveness of bullying prevention efforts in this age group. We next discuss how multidisciplinary perspectives might advance research on bullying in adolescence, with attention to one discipline (computer science, big data, and virtual communities)

Bullying can be studied within the disciplines of Computer Science, Media Studies and Anthropology. ⟵

that has already provided novel findings on bullying, and to two disciplines (media studies and anthropology) that have the potential to shape how we investigate and understand bullying. Third, to illustrate how other public health problems have been successfully addressed through multidisciplinary approaches, we provide the example of teenage pregnancy prevention and highlight how efforts from a range of disciplines have cumulatively and successfully contributed to declines in teenage pregnancy. We close with a brief summary of the origins of the special issue and an overview of the included articles.

Here, we learn that methods used to address the problem of teenage pregnancy are potentially relevant to addressing bullying in adolescence.

In Figure 13.2, we visualize the information extracted from the above introduction. You can see how bullying in adolescence can be studied by a range of disciplines, and you can also see the aspects of bullying in adolescence that can be studied to better understand and prevent it.

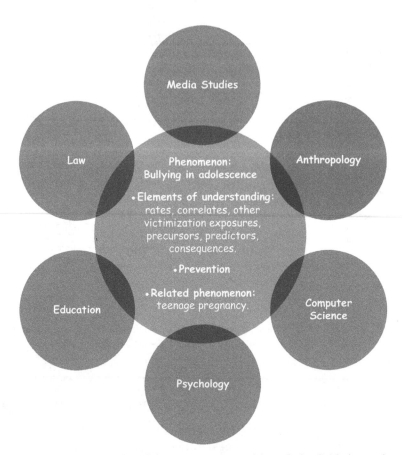

Figure 13.2 Bullying in adolescence: aspects of it and the fields it can be located within

2. What counts as knowledge in the field? (What is true according to the consensus within the field?)

Another invaluable way to understand your field is to recognize that it's composed of both problems that have been solved and problems that haven't yet been solved – or 'live' problems. In other words, there is a 'knowledge base' – the facts, as agreed upon by the experts in the field – and there are the ongoing attempts to create new knowledge.

Some fields have a large knowledge base and you'll spend most of the first few years of university study learning about this and less time exploring 'live' problems. Often, this knowledge has been empirically, or at least formally (for example, mathematically), established, and the methods for adding to the knowledge base are well developed. These fields are found in the Natural Sciences (such as Chemistry, Physics and Biology), Formal Sciences (such as Mathematics and Computer Science) and Applied Sciences (such as Engineering and Medicine) but also within the Performing and Visual Arts.

In other fields, the knowledge base is smaller, and you'll be immersed in 'live' problems from the outset. These fields are found in the Humanities (such as Philosophy and Literature) and the Social Sciences (such as Political Science and Sociology). Also, the knowledge base in such fields is not so much the facts (there may be very little that the experts agree upon other than, say, the existence of events) but rather the debates themselves; that is, having knowledge within such a field involves knowing the enduring problems within the field and the arguments made in relation to them. So, while there might be very few facts in philosophy, you would nonetheless do well to understand the key differences between Existentialists and Structuralists or between Continental and Analytic Philosophy or to understand the similarities and differences between European and Chinese philosophy. Some fields, such as Economics and Psychology, sit somewhere between the two extremes, meaning that in the early years of study there will be a balance between gaining established knowledge and exploring live problems.

An important aspect of being a critical thinker in your field is to recognize when a claim has gained the status of knowledge and when it's part of an ongoing debate. It's not always easy to do this, and sometimes we can only speak about degrees of confidence. In Figure 13.3, we show a continuum that spans from claims that are in no way supported by evidence to claims that are strongly supported by evidence. When you read, you will regularly see knowledge claims that are made with some caution.

You will find knowledge claims throughout almost everything you read. We show this in Example 13.2, which is drawn from the first

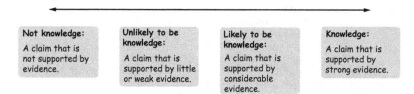

Figure 13.3   The knowledge continuum

paragraph of an Economics article, 'Toxic asset bubbles', by Ikeda and Phan (2016). As often occurs, the article begins by making largely uncontentious knowledge claims. In the remainder of the article, the authors build upon these claims by developing their own economic model to explain asset bubbles. The authors' model will be more contentious than the claims made at the start of the article. In our comments, we identify all the knowledge claims made and provide some brief commentary on them. The first paragraph of the article provides lots of useful knowledge about asset bubbles.

Example 13.2   Knowledge claims made in an introduction to an Economics article

'Toxic asset bubbles' by Ikeda and Phan (2016)

From the beginning of the introduction

The authors begin with a somewhat cautious knowledge claim. The words 'tend to follow' indicate that the authors are identifying a pattern in what often, but not always, causes financial crises. The authors provide one citation to support their claim. Despite their caution, the claim isn't very contentious and many economists would likely agree with it.

Financial crises tend to follow dramatic booms in asset prices and their collapses (Reinhart and Rogoff, 2009), especially when the booms are driven by debt financing (Minsky, 2008; Kindleberger and Aliber, 2011; Jordà et al., forthcoming). The global financial crisis of 2007–2009 that began in the USA is an illustration of such a phenomenon in which financial intermediaries are left relatively unchecked to use borrowed funds to invest in risky assets such as real estate and the associated subprime mortgage-backed securities (Reinhart and Rogoff, 2009; Rajan, 2011; Stiglitz, 2012). The role played by the combination of credit and speculation in the build-up to the crisis in the USA has also been documented by Angelides et al. (2011), Mian and Sufi (2011), and Barlevy and Fisher (2012).

This is a stronger knowledge claim than the previous one. The authors use the word 'especially' to add strength. However, as with the previous claim, this claim isn't very contentious. This claim is supported by three citations.

This is a knowledge claim about a particular historical fact. The claim that the global financial crisis of 2007-2009 began in the USA would be largely uncontested and thus has the status of knowledge.

Here, the knowledge claim is that the global financial crisis is an example of a recurring economic practice. In the two sentences, the largely uncontentious claim is supported by several citations.

3. What methods are used to create knowledge (solve problems) within the field?

Every field has its own processes or methods that it uses to create knowledge, and mastering and being able to critique these methods are very much a part of gaining expertise in your field. Much can be and is said about these methods, but we'll limit ourselves in Box 13.2 to outlining a few broad approaches. Most fields will use two or three of these methods.

Box 13.2   Common methods for creating knowledge

Formal methods

A field such as mathematics creates knowledge by building upon axioms (which are self-evident or assumed statements) using accepted rules of inference (accepted approaches to reasoning). These methods are 'formal' because they don't use 'empirical' or experimental methods; that is, all the work is done on the page. For example, Pythagoras' theorem, $a^2 + b^2 = c^2$ (the sum of the squares of the two shortest sides of a right-angle triangle equals the square of the longest side) can be proven using one of several relatively straightforward geometric techniques.

Empirical methods

Many disciplines create knowledge by systematically gathering evidence from the world itself. Empirical methods take two broad forms: quantitative and qualitative. Quantitative methods involve controlling and/or measuring variables and using statistics to analyse the data that are gathered. Examples include measuring the effect of a drug, the murder rate in a population or people's preferences about work. Qualitative methods involve gathering and analysing information that cannot be easily expressed numerically, such as responses to interview questions.

Text analysis or desk research

A considerable amount of academic work involves analysing information produced by others. We could call this 'text analysis' or 'desk research'. For example, if we study literature, we will analyse novels and poems. If we are a political scientist, we will analyse the remarks of politicians or policy documents. If we are a historian, we will analyse news articles and diary entries.

Philosophical or abstract reasoning

We also see attempts to create knowledge using philosophical or abstract reasoning. This method often combines statements about the world using logic to draw novel conclusions. An example of a straightforward 'syllogistic' argument would be:

Premise 1: I like to be treated with respect.

Premise 2: We should treat others as we would like to be treated.

Conclusion: Therefore, we should treat others with respect.

This argument is logical; however, both premises could be debated. We could ask: Do we always like to be treated with respect? And: Should we always treat others as we would like to be treated?

In some disciplines, you'll take courses about methods. As we saw above in the discussion of Question 1, this occurs in Psychology. Such courses usually cover empirical methods. In other disciplines, you build your skills in text analysis and philosophical reasoning by completing assignments; this usually occurs in subjects that are assessed with essays.

When reading, methods are sometimes explicitly addressed: in the Natural and Applied Sciences, articles usually have methods sections. Outside these areas, authors often explain how they will develop their arguments in introductions.

Examples 7.1 and 7.2, which presented introductions drawn from articles from the Arts and Sciences respectively, both clearly mentioned the methods they used. In Example 13.3, we reproduce the key sentences from both. We can see that Caron's article uses the 'Text analysis or desk research' method but that the article by Seitz et al. uses quantitative analysis.

Example 13.3   Remarks about method in two introductions

Remarks about method from the introduction from 'Silent slapstick film as ritualized clowning: the example of Charlie Chaplin' by Caron, J.E. (2006) From the introduction

This essay, however, will explore another way to understand it, one that rests on a comparison with a well-documented behavior in traditional, non-Western societies that anthropologists call ritual or sacred clowning. Examples taken from the short silent films of Charles Chaplin, specifically the two-reelers he made for Mutual Films in 1916 and 1917, will suggest that slapstick can be usefully understood as a quasi-ritualized and socially-sanctioned expression of proscribed behavior.

Remarks about method from the introduction from 'Conservation tillage and organic farming reduce soil erosion' by Seitz, S., Goebes, P., Puerta, V.L. et al. (2019)

From the introduction

This study investigated soil erosion rates under simulated heavy rainfall events in situ in the Swiss Farming System and Tillage experiment (FAST, Prechsl et al., 2017; Wittwer et al., 2017; Hartman et al., 2018), a replicated and randomized field experiment with four major arable cropping systems (organic–intensive tillage, organic–reduced tillage, conventional–intensive tillage, conventional–no tillage). Hence, we could compare these cropping systems directly without confounding factors such as differences in soil type, crop type, or crop rotation history. A portable rainfall simulator was used to dose precipitation over micro-scale runoff plots (ROP) in the field... Subsequently, sediment delivery after simulated rainfall events was collected. This method has proven reliable in rough terrain conditions and is highly suitable to measure interrill soil erosion in replicated field experiments (Seitz, 2015).

When you read, identify the method used to create knowledge; at the same time, learn from the method and critique it. More broadly, take an interest in methodological discussions in your field. They are always present and often quite heated.

4. What are the limitations of the knowledge base? (What makes developing knowledge challenging?)

This challenging question follows from the first three. In any field, there are things we'd like to know, but we haven't yet worked out how to know them. Fields move forward by recognizing the limitations of the knowledge base and devising methods to overcome these limitations.

A common challenging question that spans many disciplines is: How can we tell when a particular behaviour is a consequence of genetics and when it is a consequence of social conditioning? (This is relevant to the synthesis activity at the end of the previous chapter.) This question is challenging because it is difficult to devise methods that allow us to separate the two major influences on behaviour.

A challenging question in the Built Environment is: How do we know how a building will be experienced by its inhabitants before we build it? It is very important to know this because a lot of resources are spent producing structures; however, it is not until the structure is completed that people really get a sense of what it is like to be inside it.

A challenging question in Engineering is: How do we produce materials that are both light and strong so that we can do things like creating a space elevator that saves us from having to launch rockets? Making such materials has so far proved elusive.

If you want to learn about challenging questions in Mathematics, type 'List of unsolved problems in Mathematics' into Wikipedia and you'll find a plethora of mathematical problems. For more mathematical fun, type 'Hilbert's Problems' into Wikipedia to learn about what has probably been the most famous list of mathematical problems ever devised.

When reading, be attentive to when authors mention these kinds of challenges.

5. What is the history of the field?

To gain expertise in your field, it is invaluable not just to understand the current state of knowledge, the methods used and so on, but also to understand where your field came from. This is important because what is done today is often the result of decisions made in the past. This history includes the following:

- the origins of the field
- significant events in the field
- important figures in the field and
- how the field has changed.

At the time of writing this book, there are significant debates about the use of statistics in many of the natural and especially the applied sciences. For example, there are conventions relating to how we determine whether something like a drug has an effect; however, many are arguing that these conventions are unnecessarily rigid and lend themselves to corrupt practices (see, for example, Gunsalus et al., 2019). Anyone involved in the debate needs to understand when and why these conventions arose and their place in the broader scientific community.

Once again, you can explore the history of your subject by reading introductory texts and Wikipedia articles. However, you'll also find references to a subject's history throughout most academic articles and books, especially in introductions and literature reviews. Example 13.4 is drawn from the field of Artificial Intelligence (AI) and Law. It reproduces the first two sentences from the introduction to the article 'An empirical investigation of reasoning with legal cases through theory construction and application' by Chorley and Bench-Capon (2005). As sometimes occurs, the article introduces its subject through a brief discussion of the subject's history. In the introduction, we learn that, in the early days of applying AI to law, researchers recognized that it wasn't enough to 'formalize' legislation (in computer code); legislation had to be interpreted through reference to cases. Knowing about this early realization would no doubt help a student to understand contemporary research decisions as well as the challenges faced when using AI within Law.

Example 13.4   An introduction that takes a historical angle

'An empirical investigation of reasoning with legal cases through theory construction and application' by Chorley and Bench-Capon (2005)

From the beginning of the introduction

The importance of cases in legal reasoning has been recognised throughout the development of AI and Law. Even approaches which took formalisation of legislation as their starting point, e.g., Sergot et al. (1986), rapidly came to realise that crucial questions of the interpretation and application of terms found in the legislation could be answered only by reference to cases (e.g., Bench-Capon, 1991b).

This phrase indicates that history is being discussed.

---

6. What are the important debates within the field? Have these debates always been present or are they new?

As we've already discussed, a field is constituted not just by the knowledge within it but by current attempts to create knowledge. In most places where knowledge is being created, there are debates. These will span methodological concerns, arguments about causation, the interpretation of data and texts, the significance of findings, the worthiness of research and so on. It's important to be aware of these debates as often they will direct you to the most significant problems in a field – problems that you might like to explore. Related to this, as we saw in Chapter 2, if you want to score high marks, then exploring current debates is often a good way to go. When you are reading, contrasting perspectives are often introduced with a transition signal such as 'whereas' or 'however'.

Example 13.5 is drawn from early in the article 'Natural Capital Depletion: The Impact of Natural Disasters on Inclusive Growth' by Rajapaksa et al. (2017) from the journal *Economics of Disasters and Climate Change*. The debate that is presented relates to the question of whether natural disasters cause or hinder economic growth. There are three perspectives: (1) Natural disasters reduce economic growth. (2) Natural disasters cause economic growth. (3) One cannot generalize about the impact of natural disasters on economic growth. Note the use of 'whereas' and 'Many other studies' to indicate the different positions.

Example 13.5　A debate is presented

'Natural Capital Depletion: the Impact of Natural Disasters on Inclusive Growth' by Rajapaksa, Islam, and Managi (2017).

From early in the introduction

In a study closely related to ours, Bergholt and Lujala (2012) found that the causality between natural disasters and economic growth is negative, whereas other researchers have shown it to be positive (Fomby et al., 2013). Many other studies have provided evidence that the growth impact of natural disasters is nonlinear (Schumacher and Strobl, 2011). It is obvious that natural disasters destroy man-made and natural capital. Subsequently, the man-made capital is replenished, which is made possible through greater extraction of natural capital, unless the country is able to rebuild its man-made capital with higher efficiency.

This transition signal indicates that a contrasting perspective will follow.

This indicates that an additional perspective will be presented.

7. What are the key concepts and theories within the field?

By understanding the concepts and theories within your field, you will be able to assimilate information quickly and communicate efficiently with other members of the field.

A concept is an abstract idea that helps us to talk about some aspect of the world without having to explain the aspect in detail. In Example 13.5, we saw two concepts being used: 'man-made capital' and 'natural capital'.

'Man-made capital' refers to things of value that are created by humans, whereas 'natural capital' refers to things of value that exist in nature. Clearly, both concepts are extremely useful in efficiently discussing the economic impact of natural disasters.

A theory is an account of the way the world functions. Theories help us to make predictions and also help us to control the world. For example, Einstein's theory of relativity tells us that gravity bends space and time such that objects that are farther from a gravity source will experience more time relative to objects closer to the gravity source. Thus, a clock orbiting earth will tick faster than a clock on earth. Knowing this allows us to benefit from technologies such as GPS (Global Positioning System), which we use every day in our phones and GPS watches.

When reading, you will regularly come across unfamiliar concepts and theories. Look them up and try to understand what they mean and how they are useful in the field.

8. What other fields is the field related to? What is similar and different between the related fields? What critiques do the related fields make of one another?

Fields exist at least in part because one person cannot do everything. They allow us to specialize: to build knowledge and understanding about an area so that we can do useful things in that area, such as solve problems. However, as we mentioned earlier in the chapter, fields invariably overlap. This occurs not just because fields are always changing but because the world itself isn't neatly broken into discrete fields: the universe is much more integrated! In light of these things, it is always helpful to identify how fields overlap and think about how the expertise in one field can complement the expertise in another field. It also sometimes happens that a field becomes stagnant or even corrupt (see the discussion of the use of statistics in Example 6.1) and can be invigorated by the work in a related field. This can be described as *interdisciplinary* research: work that incorporates insights, concepts, theories and methods (amongst other things) from two or more fields.

When you are reading, look out for when other fields are mentioned. We saw this in Example 13.1, where the authors, who were interested in bullying in adolescence, argued that the problem can be addressed not only within the expected fields of Psychology and Education but also within Media Studies, Anthropology and Computer Science.

9. What does the future hold for your field? (What problems will it explore?)

To be across your field, you should also have a sense of where your field is going. For example, a new area of study might have appeared within which many discoveries will be possible. This can occur when a new technology is developed or when a theoretical innovation occurs. To use an earlier example, Einstein's theory of relativity was a theoretical innovation that led to innumerable studies and changed the way we think about the universe. By thinking about the future, you will be well placed to be a part of it. In your reading, sources will not mention the future as much as they mention the past, but you will see the occasional mention. Interestingly, at one point, Freud stated that psychoanalysis would be made obsolete by our understanding of the chemistry of the brain. This hasn't yet happened!

10. Where do you locate yourself within the field?

Hopefully, it's obvious from the earlier points that when you think about your field, you shouldn't do this as an observer looking in but as a member of the field itself. This movement from outside to inside often takes some years to occur. It requires not just knowledge and understanding but for you to change how you think about yourself: you need to shift from seeing yourself as being only a receiver of knowledge to being a creator of knowledge.

ACTIVITY 13.2

Identify when the 'field questions' are addressed

Read the first part of the introduction from the article 'Diversification, intensification and specialization: changing land use in Western Africa from 1800 BC to AD 1500' by Kay et al. (2019). (This article also appeared in Chapter 7.) Identify when it addresses the below questions; we don't include all the 'field questions' as some aren't relevant. Most of the questions are addressed several times. For the sake of the activity, assume that the broader field of study is anthropogenic (human-created) environmental change.

1. What does the field study? (What types of problems is the field concerned with?)

2. What counts as knowledge in the field? (What is true according the consensus within the field?)

3. What methods are used to create knowledge (solve problems) within the field?

4. What are the limitations of the knowledge base? (What makes developing knowledge challenging?)

6. What are the important debates within the field? Have these debates always been present, or are they new?

7. What are the key concepts and theories within the field? (These are often closely related to the problems and debates within the field.)

Introduction

In sub-Saharan Africa over the last four millennia, the types of societal shifts that either occurred in response to environmental change or that acted as drivers of that change include the shift to food production, the development of iron metallurgy, population growth, and the emergence of centralized states and empires. Additionally, different societies had different means of maintaining their way of life, and these livelihoods had varying effects on their local environments. The area that is used for human habitation and the procurement of food and fuel varies based on population, subsistence strategy, mobility, economy, available technology, and the intensity with which the land is used (Kay and Kaplan, 2015). Land use in turn has widely varying effects on the landscape with respect to vegetation composition (Höhn and Neumann, 2012; Mwampamba and Schwartz, 2011; Zeidler et al., 2002); biogeochemical cycling (Kaplan, Krumhardt et al. 2010; Vitousek et al., 1997); erosion (Ciampalini et al., 2012; De Brue and Verstraeten, 2014; Vanwalleghem et al., 2017); fire regimes (Battistel et al., 2017; Pfeiffer et al., 2013); and hydrology (Russell et al., 2009; Xing et al., 2014).

Deforestation and species extinction are the most commonly cited examples of human influence on the environment in sub-Saharan Africa (e.g., Fairhead and Leach, 1995, 1996; Norris et al., 2010), and at least one study has shown that present-day patterns of tree cover are more strongly controlled by human land use than by climate (Aleman et al., 2016). However, the implications of human land use are not necessarily negative and there are several examples of sustainable agricultural practices or other forms of beneficial land management that might preserve or increase biodiversity (e.g., Backes, 2001; Butzer, 1996; Denevan, 1995; Fairhead and Leach, 1996; Heckenberger et al., 2007; Niemeijer, 1996), or even mitigate climate change (Solomon et al., 2016).

How humans influenced their environment in the past and when that influence began are thus topics of vigorous debate (e.g., Ellis et al., 2016; Fischer-Kowalski et al., 2014; Foley et al., 2013; Kaplan et al., 2016; Lewis and Maslin, 2015; Ruddiman, 2005; Smith and Zeder, 2013; Vanwalleghem et al., 2017). In some parts of the world, these effects are easily detected, because of the relatively recent arrival of humans on the landscape (e.g., Douglass and Zinke, 2015; McWethy et al., 2009), or the unmistakable impact of urbanization and extractive industries (e.g., Kaplan et al., 2011; Uglietti et al., 2015). In other areas, the line between natural climate-driven change and human niche construction is harder to define (e.g., Braje and Erlandson, 2013; Glikson, 2013; Wright, 2017). It has even been proposed that the development of pastoral economies in the Sahara may have had consequences for the end of the African Humid Period c. 8,000–4,500 years ago, either hastening it (Wright, 2017) or conversely delaying it (Brierley et al., 2018).

Conclusion

All students are aware that there are different areas of study. We learn this in our school days when we study different subjects, such as mathematics, physics, literature and so on. However, many leave school and enter university with the rather unhelpful assumption that to study a subject involves little more than learning what counts as knowledge within it. A successful university student will not just learn the knowledge within their field, they'll learn about their field's history, the 'live' problems within it, the techniques used for solving these problems and so on. Gaining this mastery will allow you to succeed both within the university and in your future work outside university. To gain mastery of your field, you should immerse yourself in your field. Go to your classes, do at least a portion of your set readings, give yourself time to develop your responses to assignment questions and, importantly, always keep in mind the questions in Box 13.1.

14

Reading to Write: Developing Your Own Academic Voice by Imitating Good Writers

Introduction

The purpose of this chapter is to encourage you to learn to become a good writer by observing how experienced writers write. When you read academic sources, you shouldn't focus only on information; you should also pay attention to the ways that authors present and analyse information. In doing this and using similar techniques, you'll effectively be ensuring that your own critical voice is present in your writing. We encourage you to develop your own collection of useful phrases. To help you get started, we'll provide you with a range of categories that you can populate with the phrases you find.

We'll finish the chapter by saying some more about 'academic voice'. We'll explain that you need to strike a balance between having too much voice and not enough voice. When your voice isn't sufficiently present, you'll be in danger of plagiarizing.

So, what does academic writing look like?

Hopefully, you've now got a very good sense of what academic writing looks like! But to clarify, there is a general pattern in what takes place in academic articles and books. It is this: in the introduction, a problem is introduced that needs to be solved. This can be a specific problem, such as whether a new drug works, or an open-ended problem, such as learning what life is present in an unexplored part of the ocean. In the body, the details of the solution are presented with an emphasis on providing evidence to support the claims that are made. In the conclusion, what has been achieved is summarized and the (or a) solution to the problem is clarified. Within each of these stages, many different activities can occur, as we have already pointed out in Box 7.2 ('Reading for the "bumps": six questions that will help you work out what a source is about') and Box 10.1 ('Some ways of using information you find in your sources'). (The information in these boxes complements the information in this chapter.)

Introductions

Broadly, introductions clarify *what* you are going to focus on (the subject and the specific problem within the subject), *why* the subject and problem are significant, and *how* you'll go about solving your problem. Details are provided in Box 14.1.

Box 14.1   The things that occur within introductions

Typical functions within introductions	Example of language used
Introducing the subject and its significance	– X has been the focus of much research in recent years because of its significance in …
Introducing the central problem or question and its significance	– However, X remains a major cause of illness, and we have not yet developed an adequate response.
Introducing the purpose of the work	– The purpose of the study is to …
Additional introduction functions	**Example of language used**
Stating the general argument to be made (the thesis)	– We argue that X is best addressed by doing Y.
Stating a hypothesis to be tested	– This study will test the hypothesis that increasing Y will cause Z.
Clarifying and justifying the scope of the discussion	– Although we could explore W, X, Y or Z, the current study will focus on Y because …

Presenting an overview of the method to solve the problem, answer the question or test the hypothesis	– To determine whether the intervention was justified, four key documents will be analysed.
Defining key terms	– In this paper, we understand X to mean ...
Outlining how the work will be structured	– First, a background to X will be provided. Second, three suspected causes of X will be outlined and assessed. Third, ...
Providing an overview of relevant literature	– There have been three perspectives on X. First, ...
Presenting a current debate	– The utility of X continues to be debated. On the one hand, ...
Providing a history	– X was first studied in 1952 ...
Mentioning the inadequacies or gaps within previous research	– Although previous research has explored X, its treatment of Y has been inadequate.

You can look over the examples in Chapter 7 to see which of the functions in Box 14.1 occur. We won't provide analysis here as our analysis would be similar to that in Chapter 7.

In the body of a work

There are many different things that are done in the body of a work. In empirical work, methods and results are presented and discussed; in contrast, in essayistic work, arguments are made, supported by evidence from other sources. Box 14.2 introduces many of these things. You can search for some of these functions in Activity 14.1.

Box 14.2 The things that occur within body paragraphs

Typical functions within a body paragraph	Example of language used
Introducing the topic of the paragraph (plus linking and justification)	– Having considered X, we now need to assess Y because ...
Clarifying a focus	– With respect to X, ...

Referring to an earlier discussion	– Closely related to the previous point, ... – As mentioned earlier, ...
Indicating a sequence of points or listing	– First, Smith (2018) fails to account for ... Second, Smith claims that ...
Adding information	– Furthermore, we have seen that ... – Moreover, ...
Introducing others' work	– Saleh (2019) found that ... – Wong (2017) argues that ... – Smith (2018) claims that ...
Pointing out a similarity	– Even though Wong (2017) and Smith (2018) are ostensibly concerned with X and Y, they share ...
Introducing a counterpoint	– However, Wong (2017) found that ...
Showing contrasting perspectives	– Saleh (2019) argues X ... However, Smith (2018) suggests that ...
Providing an example	– An excellent example of X is ...
Summing up or concluding	– In sum, although X appears useful, it fails to ... – Given X and Y, we can conclude that ...
Being critical	– Although X does an excellent job of ..., it lacks ...
Analysing	– From these examples, we can see that ...
Showing caution when making a claim	– It is likely that X causes Y. – Generally, we see that ...
Describing others' methods	– Previously, researches have attempted to understand X by doing Y.
Describing your method	– Three techniques were used to test the purity of X. First, ...
Discussing results	– We found X. This is surprising given that previous research indicated that ...

ACTIVITY 14.1

Identifying functions within body paragraphs

Below is a paragraph drawn from the article, 'Anger, provocation and loss of self-control: what does "losing it" really mean?' by Sarah Sorial from the journal *Criminal Law and Philosophy* (2019). See which typical functions of a body paragraph you can identify; note the language used. Our analysis is in the back of the book. So that the paragraph makes sense, we've included the abstract from the article (you don't need to analyse this).

Abstract (don't analyse this!)

Drawing on recent research in the philosophy of the emotions and empirical evidence from social psychology, this paper argues that the concept of loss of self-control at common law mischaracterises the relationship between the emotions and their effects on action. Emotions do not undermine reason in the ways offenders describe (and courts sometimes accept); nor do they compel people to act in ways they cannot control. As such, the idea of 'loss of self-control' is an inaccurate and misleading description of the psychological mechanisms at play in cases of emotionally motivated killing, where there may not be any 'loss of self-control' as such.

Body paragraph (analyse this)

Third, it is not clear why the law shows lenience to human frailty in some cases but not in others. For example, as Baron notes, we do not mitigate robbery when we discover that the defendant was an addict and stole money to buy his drugs; nor is there a partial defence for those who steal money to pay the rent to avoid eviction and the fate of living with their young children on the streets. Both these cases involve human frailty, and the case of the drug addict involves loss of self-control in ways that can be easily explained and understood, given what we know about the state of mind of the addict and of compulsion more generally. And yet, we do not accept these as mitigating factors. The idea of loss of self-control is thus applied inconsistently, and provides a concession to only some forms of human frailty, namely, those frailties traditionally associated with ideas about masculinity.

Conclusions

Conclusions have two main purposes. They summarize what occurred in the work, and they state the solution to the problem that was being addressed. This can be a claim or 'thesis' that all of your arguments have been supporting, a statement about whether a hypothesis has been confirmed or refuted, or something similar. Conclusions – usually for empirical work – can do additional things such as mention the significance of what has been argued or found or deficiencies in the work and, most commonly, suggest future research (Box 14.3).

Box 14.3   The things that occur within conclusions

Typical functions within conclusions	Example of language used
Reminding the reader of your purpose	– The purpose of this paper was to ...
Summarizing what occurred	– Three arguments in favour of X were assessed. First, ...
Presenting the main finding or argument	– Our experiment demonstrated that X has a significant impact on ... – From these points, we can conclude that ...
Additional functions within conclusions	**Example of language used**
Mentioning significance	– The results are significant because ...
Pointing out deficiencies in the work	– Although we can claim with confidence that ..., the study didn't sufficiently ...
Suggesting further research	– Given the limitations of the present study, future research could ...

ACTIVITY 14.2

Identifying functions within conclusions

This conclusion is drawn from the article, 'Conservation tillage and organic farming reduce soil erosion' by Seitz, Goebes, Puerta, et al. (2019). The introduction to this article appeared in Chapter 7. Once again, identify the different functions in the conclusion and note the language used. Answers are in the back of the book.

Conclusion

This study enabled ranking four different arable cropping systems regarding soil erosion and showed for the first time in situ that the application of reduced tillage in organic farming can further decrease sediment delivery. Thus, it appears to be a major improvement for soil erosion control in organic farming systems. The experiment demonstrated that reduced soil erosion in organic agriculture compared to conventional agriculture was mainly driven by soil surface cover and SOM. Additionally, this work showed that a living plant cover from weeds can reduce soil erosion more effectively compared to dead plant residues in conventional, no-tillage systems.

Further research is required on factors influencing soil erosion in organic farming systems in order to apply them generally. Such research should include other types of organic farming with different cultivation and manure regimes on different substrates and within different climates. It should also cover the influences of microorganisms on aggregation, especially the impact of arbuscular mycorrhizal fungi (AMF), a group of soil fungi known to influence soil structure (van der Heijden et al., 2006). Finally, it is of high interest to conduct further research on the effects of reduced tillage techniques on different types of organic farming systems and their individual application in different environments (Cooper et al., 2016). In this context, the consideration of reduced tillage within strategies to increase yields in organic farming becomes of importance, as those strategies will most of all contribute to the general acceptance of organic principles in farming (Röös et al., 2018).

Your academic voice and plagiarism

As mentioned, being conscious of all the above elements of academic writing while you read will help you to become a better writer because when you employ these elements in your writing, you'll be developing your own academic voice. Without an academic voice, you'll struggle to get good marks. We'll now explore voice in more detail by considering what it means to have too much voice (yes, this is also an issue!) and not enough voice. Having not enough voice is a serious problem because it often amounts to plagiarism.

Having too much voice

Assignments that have too much voice do not sufficiently engage with others' work. We saw this mentioned in Boxes 3.1 and 3.2 where we provided an overview of marking criteria. Relevant comments include that poor assignments contain little or no evidence of reading/research and make many unsubstantiated generalizations. These problems can usually be traced to a student struggling to understand the course material or laziness. A lazy student will respond to an assignment question by writing 'off the top of their head'. Their points will often be superficial and possibly dubious because they won't have exposed themselves to the work of experts in their field who have spent years researching and thinking about similar problems.

Having not enough voice: the problem of plagiarism

Assignments with not enough voice are dominated by quotations, summaries and paraphrases that are not integrated into the student's argument. In fact, the student might not even have an argument; rather, they simply present a collage of others' work. In the worst cases, sources of information are not even acknowledged with a citation. Here, the student is effectively deceiving the reader about their voice: they are passing others' voices off as their own.

Students can have trouble developing their own voice when they are struggling with the course material. The student may well be capable of finding relevant sources; however, because they are struggling, they are unable to form their own opinions and thus are unable to do anything meaningful with the information they find. Students struggle with course material for several reasons. In the worst case, the student is not capable of engaging with the material since they lack the necessary prior education. A lack of interest can also play a big role.

A second reason students have trouble developing their voice is because they have the wrong state of mind when reading. If the student is being overly passive and just reading to absorb information rather than reading comparatively or asking themselves what they think about the material, then when it comes time to write they'll struggle to do much more than reproduce others' ideas.

A third reason is that the student hasn't paid attention in class and hasn't spent enough time reading, making notes, planning and drafting. It takes time for anyone to develop meaningful ideas about a topic.

Finally, even strong students can lose their voice when writing. Often, they have read a lot and want to cram as much of it as they can into their assignments, but in doing so, they forsake topic sentences, reporting phrases, transition signals and analysis.

To finish, we want to stress that even if you are struggling to come up with your own original ideas in an assignment, you can still score very high marks by employing synthesis: by leading your reader through the ideas of others and pointing out which perspectives you find more or less compelling.

Conclusion

When you read, don't just read for information but for how information is presented. Be attentive to all the different functions within anything you read, and note how these functions are signalled. If you do this for a few months and build your own collection of useful phrases, your own writing will improve substantially. Ultimately, you will be ensuring that your voice is present in your assignments.

Reading Widely to Enrich Your Studies and Life

Introduction

Up to this point, we've encouraged you to be strategic when you read. Our goal has been to help you reduce your reading time while increasing the sophistication of your engagement with your sources. However, there's another type of reading that deserves a mention: reading widely.

By 'reading widely', we mean reading (or indeed watching) anything that isn't narrowly linked with your course or, say, dissertation topic. We are talking about novels, articles, books on specialized topics for a general audience, classic movies and so on. Whereas reading strategically will help you master your area of study, reading widely will make you a more rounded individual – as they say – and will likely provide your studies and professional and private life with unexpected benefits. Once again, we can use the letter 'T' to illustrate what we are talking about. The vertical part of the 'T' represents your specialization; this relates to your strategic reading. The horizontal part represents your general knowledge; this relates to your wider reading. In this brief chapter, we'll discuss some of the benefits of reading widely and give some simple advice about how to do it.

The benefits of reading widely

Enriching your field by incorporating material from beyond it

Fields or disciplines exist in part because individual expertise is limited: an individual can master only a certain amount of knowledge and gain a certain number of skills in their lifetime. Discipline boundaries demarcate a space within which experts can work together to solve similar problems. Although discipline boundaries help us to focus on problems, these boundaries can sometimes limit the resources we draw upon to solve problems. They can also lead to stagnation, where a discipline continues to use questionable approaches because doing so is the norm. Our simple point is that if you practice your discipline with an open mind – a mind enriched by learning from many areas – you'll gain many unexpected benefits.

For example, many feminist scholars of world politics consider Cynthia Enloe's *Bananas, Beaches and Bases: Making Feminist Sense of International Politics* (2000 [1989]) to be a ground-breaking work. For much of the twentieth century, gender rarely, if ever, was explicitly studied in the context of world politics; it was seen as simply irrelevant. Even when feminist scholars began to undertake this work, it was still seen as peripheral to the 'serious' issues of world politics and potentially risky for one's career. (Joshua Goldstein, the author of *War and Gender: How Gender Shapes the War System and Vice Versa* [2001], for example, wrote 'Recently, I discovered a list of unfinished research projects, which I had made fifteen years ago at the end of graduate school. About ten lines down is "gender and war", with the notation "most interesting of all; will ruin career – wait until tenure"' [2001].) What was especially remarkable about Enloe's book (and the many of hers that have followed, including *The Curious Feminist* and *The Big Push*) was how she drew from areas that had never been considered in world politics scholarship, because, being part of the 'domestic' or 'personal' sphere, they weren't even considered to fall within the realm of world politics. So, for example, she turned her analytical gaze to flight attendants and chambermaids, to sunny beaches and factories producing jeans, and to Carmen Miranda and the international banana trade. She sees the 'political' in the 'domestic' and demonstrates that, far from being an apolitical realm, the domestic and the personal are just as political as the boardrooms and military bases.

On a more modest scale, incorporating material from beyond your field can make your writing more interesting. It demonstrates that you can think beyond the narrow confines of your field, make connections between different ideas and give the reader a more enjoyable and meaningful reading experience. For example, if you were exploring the phenomenon of 'confirmation bias' in an essay, you might – in addition to exploring what Psychologists say on the matter – quote Laurence Sterne's eighteenth-century novel, *The Life and Opinions of Tristram Shandy, Gentleman*: 'It is the nature of an hypothesis, when once a man has conceived it, that it assimilates every thing to itself, as proper nourishment; and, from the first moment of your begetting it, it generally grows the stronger by every thing you see, hear, read, or understand.'

When reading widely, don't underestimate the power of serendipity. You might not immediately see the links between disparate fields, but beneficial connections will almost always arise. Both of us benefited in our respective PhD dissertations from reading widely.

Meeting interesting people by being interesting

A considerable component of many professional lives involves not just doing one's job but socializing with other professionals. Although doing your job well will certainly help you succeed, being an interesting person who is able to converse on a range of topics will also make a difference. So, take an interest in nineteenth-century French literature, watch the movies of Kurosawa, read some classic Chinese philosophical texts and visit your local art gallery once in a while. It's all good for you.

The change in direction

Whereas some people stay in the same field their whole lives, for others this is neither desirable nor indeed possible. If, for whatever reason, you need to leave your field and move on to something else, then the interests you've developed through reading widely might lead you to a new hobby or career or will at least bring a little diversity to your life!

How to read (and watch) widely

It's not hard to find interesting things to read and watch. All of the following work.

1. Listen out for recommendations from people you respect. Often, in a digression, a university teacher will tell you about a classic book, movie or TV show. Follow their recommendation, especially if you hear one or two others recommend the same thing. Also follow the recommendations of reviewers you respect.
2. When reading for your courses and assignments, keep an eye out for interesting references.
3. Google things like 'the best books in Structural Engineering'. Read a few lists, then pick a title and start reading.

Conclusion

The main point you should take away from this book is that successful reading at university is multifaceted. An inexperienced, passive reader will simply read to absorb information. But even when such a reader reads a lot, they will still struggle to produce decent assignments. This is because they are not thinking, while they are reading, about all the things they can do with others' work. As we have demonstrated, there are, in fact, a vast amount of things you can do with what you read. You might treat a source as authoritative and use it to support a claim, or you might treat it as an object of study and analyse it to reveal something interesting about society. You might strengthen an argument you are making by showing how an author is mistaken in an argument they themselves make or you might combine the information in one source with the information from another source to produce something new. The list goes on and on. You certainly won't be a masterful reader when you begin your studies, but if you continue to immerse yourself in your discipline and consult this book from time to time, soon enough your reading will be directed by dozens of useful questions, and you won't even have to think about it – it will just happen.

Answers

Activity 4.1 Answers

- *The Victorian Web* is an unusual source. As explained on one of its pages, there is a conscientious review process, and most of the contributors are academics. However, given that it isn't a standard academic journal, you should assess the merits of individual articles before including them in an assignment; amongst other things, determine the credentials of the author and scrutinize how well they substantiate their claims. Also, although it may be acceptable in an assignment to draw on one or two sources from the site, you shouldn't rely heavily on it; that is, ensure that the majority of your sources come from peer-reviewed journals and books. In short, you can treat some of the articles as authoritative but with caution.

- *The United Nations Convention on the Rights of the Child* is a non-standard source that can be used in a variety of ways. You could treat it as authority if you were critiquing the practices of a country in relation to children. However, if you did this, you shouldn't assume that everything in the *Convention* is right; that is, you should be aware of the debates surrounding the use of the *Convention*. You could also treat the *Convention* as an object of study; that is, you could analyse it to reveal useful information, such as current assumptions about the rights of children.

- *Time Magazine* isn't an academic source. It has a reasonable reputation and cites its sources. However, it is produced for a popular, not an academic, audience. And it's unclear how recent (as of 2018) changes in ownership will affect its content. You would likely not treat it as authority. However, it might be a useful source for information such as quotations. It could also be a useful object of study. For example, if you were writing an assignment about the media's depictions of a notable individual and *Time* wrote about that individual, given the prominence of *Time*, it might be worth analysing the article.

Activity 7.1 Our analysis

1. Subject. This is the broader subject within which the specific subject of the article sits.

1. Subject. This is the specific subject of the article, as announced in the title.

Many societal and environmental changes occurred between the 2nd millennium BC and the middle of the 2nd millennium AD in western Africa. Key amongst these were changes in land use due to the spread and development of agricultural strategies, which may have had widespread consequences for the climate, hydrology, biodiversity, and ecosystem services of the region. However, quantification of these land-use influences and potential feedbacks between human and natural systems is controversial, in part because the archaeological and historical record is highly fragmented in time and space.

3. Significance of the subject.

2. Problem.

To improve our understanding of how humans contributed to the development of African landscapes, we developed an atlas of land-use practices in western Africa for nine time-windows over the period 1800 BC to AD 1500. The maps are based on a broad synthesis of archaeological, archaeobotanical, archaeozoological, historical, linguistic, genetic, and ethnographic data and present land use in 12 basic categories. The main differences between categories is the relative reliance on, and variety of, domesticated plant and animal species utilized and the energy invested in cultivating or keeping them. The maps highlight the irregular and frequently non-linear trajectory of land-use change in the prehistory of western Africa. Representing an original attempt to produce rigorous spatial synthesis from diverse sources, the atlas will be useful for a range of studies of human–environment interactions in the past and highlight major spatial and temporal gaps in data that may guide future field studies.

4. Method. This is the overview of how the problem was addressed.

4. Method. Details of the method are provided.

5. Solution. A notable aspect of the project is articulated.

3. Significance of the project.

Answers for the Chapter 11 activity

Focus question: What are some problems with the normal avenues of academic publishing? How could academic publishing be done differently?

What is the significance of the question and what are your tentative responses?

Academic publishing is an important but tricky business. There are always more people wanting to be published than publishers are willing to accept. Thus, there must be a vetting process. And even the best work usually needs to be revised before publishing. Within this vetting and revising process, many problems arise. The process is often lengthy, and there is always the question of whether the best work gets published. Then there are concerns about the accuracy of published material. Also, there is debate about the reputations of journals and publishers, and how universities regard various journals and publishers, which can have a bearing on researchers' careers.

Which aspects of the article are relevant?

In the article, in the section titled 'Openness', Bargmann makes some clear contributions to the discussion. First, she comments on the speed of academic publishing. When talking about her time spent researching *Caenorhabditis elegans*, she mentions that results were published semi-regularly in the *Worm Breeder's Gazette*. This 'news-letter' was not a peer-reviewed academic journal and yet it was remarkably successful. She states that results could be published in weeks or months rather than years, as is the case with normal academic publishing in peer-reviewed journals.

Second, and related to this, she makes a useful contribution to the discussion of peer review. Given that the *Worm Breeder's Gazette* was not peer-reviewed, the broader scientific community might be concerned that false knowledge claims were being published. She makes the simple point that 'results that can't be replicated soon get ignored'. This is potentially a major critique of the peer-review process. We could ask: do we actually need peer review – can we rely, instead, on replication? There is much to say here; however, we must move on!

Third, she addresses the idea that the only way to claim ownership of your results is to have them 'formally' published in a peer-reviewed journal. With respect to the *Worm Breeder's Gazette*, she states, 'As for stealing others' work, I think that the very openness of the *C. elegans* field acted as a deterrent. Everyone knew what was in the *WBG*, and there was a clear expectation that if you used someone else's result, you included that person in your study or cited them.' Her point is that faster, less formal publications do not lead to the theft of ideas. This point would be debatable in a commercial context.

Fourth, she addresses the possibility that the less open nature of normal academic publishing is not conducive to knowledge creation. We imagine that, in the 'normal' context, people work in isolated groups on particular problems, guarding their results from competing groups until they are formally published. This, when combined (we assume) with the slowness of academic publishing, can lead to similar work being conducted in an uncoordinated manner. In contrast, the 'open' nature of publishing characterized by the *WBG* meant that 'people could find out in advance whether similar work was in progress in another lab, and coordinate publications'.

We see Bargmann's critiques of normal academic publishing returning via implication in the section 'Shaping science today' when she states that 'we at the Chan Zuckerberg Initiative want all of biomedical science to be faster, more robust, sharable and scalable'. Both 'faster' and 'sharable' imply critiques of the slow and less cooperative nature of normal academic publishing. She explores 'sharable' in more detail later in the article when speaking again about 'openness', making points similar to those already discussed.

You will notice that even though Bargmann doesn't dedicate very many words to exploring the relative merits of non-traditional and normal avenues of academic publishing, we were able to extract a lot of excellent information because we read with a well-developed filter in mind.

How could the relevant information in the article be used?

Bargmann's remarks can be used in two main ways. First, Bargmann introduces us to four significant aspects of – or topics within – academic publishing: the speed of publication, the question of accuracy, the ownership of discoveries and the problem of cooperation. There are more topics to discuss; however, if we were producing, say, a 2,000-word assignment, we could certainly dedicate a paragraph to each of the above topics.

Second, Bargmann provides some controversial perspectives. These would be great to analyse; specifically, it would be useful to consider when her perspectives were justified and when they were problematic. For example, the idea that replication can be a substitute for peer review is pleasantly romantic; however, it is probably feasible within only a small research community. If peer review were broadly dispensed with, sloppy researchers and charlatans the world over would publish poor work and gain unfair benefits from doing so.

You can see that we are not treating Bargmann's ideas as definitive. Instead, we are using them to identify significant topics for discussion and interesting perspectives within these topics. We'd expect to consult more articles before we wrote up our response to the question.

Focus question: Which is superior, youth or age?

What is the significance of the question and what are your tentative responses?

The question of which is superior, youth or age, is a frequently encountered broad question. It's sometimes openly debated, but even when it isn't, people have strong, often unexamined, opinions about it. In popular movies and music, youth is often preferred to age. However, with respect to employment, the young (16–24) sometimes struggle to find work because of a lack of experience. Similarly, in education and research, it is often assumed that age is superior to youth because of experience. Yet given that older people often have more power and wealth than younger people, we could hypothesize that, in some instances, the older generation protects its power and wealth in part by using spurious claims about superiority.

Which aspects of the article are relevant?

Bargmann doesn't say much on this question, but she makes one remarkable point. In the section 'Shaping science today' when discussing how she hopes to foster creativity in the Chan Zuckerberg Science Initiative, she writes, 'to foster creativity, we plan to support people who want to work in new areas – especially young researchers setting up their own labs. Most scientists do their most creative work at this early stage of their careers.' In saying this, Bargmann challenges the assumption that age is superior to youth. She also alludes to the phenomenon of 'gatekeeping'. This is when older, established professionals limit access to their field, restricting those who do not conform to their agenda. She writes, 'disease-relevant fields can be some of the hardest to break into for someone with a new idea or approach.'

How could the relevant information in the article be used? Does the article confirm, expand or challenge what you already think?

We could use Bargmann's claim about the success of young researchers in a broader discussion of innovation. This discussion would in turn be just one of many discussions in relation to the question. Given that Bargmann doesn't provide any evidence, we could attempt to substantiate her claim by finding statistics or perhaps more creatively by seeing whether psychologists have found that younger people are perhaps

Activity 12.2 Our synthesis

This topic sentence introduces the question to be addressed in the paragraph and indicates the significance of the topic.

This provides a broad outline of what will occur in the paragraph. Both this and the previous sentence show that we have good general understanding of the topic.

Given the three sources that discuss specific intelligences share the same perspective, we simply made sure that each source was represented in our synthesis (there was no need to contrast and evaluate).

The question of whether there are sex differences in intelligence has been debated for millennia and continues to engage both researchers and the general public. Surveying the literature, we can respond to this question in three ways. First, we can consider the commonly used construct, 'general intelligence'. Many researchers argue that there is no difference in general intelligence between women and men (see Burgaleta, 2012; Liu and Lynn, 2014; Halpern, 2000; Brody, 1992), whereas some argue that there is a slight difference favouring men (van der Linden et al., 2017) and suggest that the larger average total brain volume could be the contributing factor. Second, we can consider specific intelligences; this may well be a better way to proceed given the variety of tasks that humans perform. There is considerable evidence that men and women excel at different tasks (Liu and Lynn, 2014). Men tend to perform better at what Burgaleta et al. (2012) refer to as 'visuospatial abilities' and mathematical reasoning (Kimura, 2002), whereas women perform better at such tasks as recalling and identifying words, matching items and precision manual tasks (Kimura, 2002). Third, we can consider the distribution of intelligence within the two groups. There is some evidence that men have a broader distribution than women (Deary et al., 2010; Penrose, 1963), which means that there will be more men with very low general intelligence than women but also more men with very high general intelligence than women. In sum, it seems that with respect to general intelligence, average differences between men and women are either very small or non-existent. However, there do seem to be differences in specific intelligences and in the distribution of intelligence within each group. Notably, we have said little about the potential causes of any differences. These causes could be biological or they could be social.

We attempt to accurately represent the difference in perspectives about general intelligence.

We add our own opinion here, which was derived from thinking about the challenges of speaking about 'general intelligence'.

We added some explanation here for the sake of clarity.

In this conclusion we present our perspective and add some thoughts about the problem of causality. In an essay we would likely tackle causality in a later section.

bolder and more speculative than older people. Bargmann's claim goes some way towards confirming our hypothesis about the older generation's questionable use of power.

Activity 13.2 Our analysis

Introduction

1. What does the field study. 6. Debate. We learn from the first lines that a major area of study is the relationship between societal shifts and environmental change in sub-Saharan Africa. It's implied that there is a debate about whether societal shifts caused or were caused by environmental change. The specifics of societal change that are studied are also mentioned.

In sub-Saharan Africa over the last four millennia, the types of societal shifts that either occurred in response to environmental change or acted as drivers of that change include the shift to food production, the development of iron metallurgy, population growth, and the emergence of centralized states and empires. Additionally, different societies had different means of maintaining their way of life and these livelihoods had varying effects on their local environments. The area that is used for human habitation and the procurement of food and fuel varies on the basis of population, subsistence strategy, mobility, economy, available technology, and the intensity with which the land is used (Kay and Kaplan, 2015). Land use in turn has widely varying effects on the landscape with respect to vegetation composition (Höhn and Neumann, 2012; Mwampamba and Schwartz, 2011; Zeidler et al., 2002); biogeochemical cycling (Kaplan, Krumhardt et al., 2010; Vitousek et al., 1997); erosion (Ciampalini et al., 2012; De Brue and Verstraeten, 2014; Vanwalleghem et al., 2017); fire regimes (Battistel et al., 2017; Pfeiffer et al., 2013); and hydrology (Russell et al., 2009; Xing et al., 2014).

2. Knowledge.

2. Knowledge. Details follow.

7. Concept.

1. What does the field study? 2. Knowledge. 7. Concept. 'Deforestation' and 'species extinction' are not just problems to be studied within the broader field of environmental change, they are also useful technical terms that you could use when researching a similar topic.

Deforestation and species extinction are the most commonly cited examples of human influence on the environment in sub-Saharan Africa (e.g., Fairhead and Leach, 1995, 1996; Norris et al. 2010), and at least one study has shown that present-day patterns of tree cover are more strongly controlled by human land use than by climate (Aleman et al., 2016). However, the implications of human land use are not necessarily negative and there are several examples of sustainable agricultural practices or other forms of beneficial land management that might preserve or increase biodiversity (e.g., Backes, 2001; Butzer, 1996; Denevan, 1995; Fairhead and Leach, 1996; Heckenberger et al., 2007; Niemeijer, 1996) or even mitigate climate change (Solomon et al. 2016).

1. What does the field study? 2. Knowledge. 6. Debate. Clearly an important question and indeed debate is whether or not human land use necessarily has a negative impact on biodiversity.

6. Debate. ←——How humans influenced their environment in the past and when that influence began are thus topics of vigorous debate (e.g., Ellis et al., 2016; Fischer-Kowalski et al., 2014; Foley et al., 2013; Kaplan et al., 2016; Lewis and Maslin, 2015; Ruddiman, 2005; Smith and Zeder, 2013; Vanwalleghem et al., 2017). In some parts of the world, these effects are easily detected because of the relatively recent arrival of humans on the landscape (e.g., Douglass and Zinke, 2015; McWethy et al., 2009) or the unmistakable impact of urbanization and extractive industries (e.g., Kaplan et al., 2011; Uglietti et al., 2015). In other areas, the line between natural climate-driven change and human niche construction is

6. Debate. ← harder to define (e.g., Braje and Erlandson, 2013; Glikson, 2013; Wright, 2017). It has even been proposed that the development of pastoral economies in the Sahara may have had consequences for the end of the African Humid Period about 8,000 to 4,500 years ago, either hastening it (Wright, 2017) or conversely delaying it (Brierley et al., 2018).

3. Method. 4. Limitations of the knowledge base. While these comments don't directly address method, they are broadly related to methodological challenges. We learn that it's hard to gain knowledge about some areas because, it is implied, humans have occupied such regions for a long time.

Activity 14.1 Our analysis

Body paragraph

Pointing out a sequence (and thus also providing a link with the previous paragraph).

Providing an example.

Analyzing ←

Third, it is not clear why the law shows lenience to human frailty in some cases but not in others. For example, as Baron notes, we do not mitigate robbery when we discover that the defendant was an addict and stole money to buy his drugs; nor is there a partial defence for those who steal money to pay the rent to avoid eviction and the fate of living with their young children on the streets. Both these cases involve human frailty, and the case of the drug addict involves loss of self-control in ways that can be easily explained and understood, given what we know about the state of mind of the addict and of compulsion more generally. And yet, we do not accept these as mitigating factors.

Concluding (note the world 'thus').

The idea of loss of self-control is thus applied inconsistently, and provides a concession to only some forms of human frailty, namely, those frailties traditionally associated with ideas about masculinity.

Introducing the topic of the paragraph (in this case, the topic is an argument).

Introducing others' work.

Introducing a similar point.

Activity 14.2 Our analysis

Conclusion

The conclusion begins by reminding us of what it did. Note the move to past tense.

This study enabled ranking four different arable cropping systems regarding soil erosion and showed for the first time *in situ* that the application of reduced tillage in organic farming can further decrease sediment delivery.

The main finding is stated. This is introduced with the words 'and showed'.

Thus, it appears to be a major improvement for soil erosion control in organic farming systems. The experiment demonstrated that reduced soil erosion in organic agriculture compared with conventional agriculture was driven mainly by soil surface cover and soil organic matter. Additionally, this work showed that a living plant cover from weeds can reduce soil erosion more effectively compared with dead plant residues in conventional, no-tillage systems.

The significance of the finding is clarified. Note this is introduced with 'thus'.

The conclusion presents the details of the solution.

Further details are presented.

Further research is required on factors influencing soil erosion in organic farming systems in order to apply them generally. Such research should include other types of organic farming with different cultivation and manure regimes on different substrates and within different climates. It should also cover the influences of microorganisms on aggregation, especially the impact of arbuscular mycorrhizal fungi (AMF), a group of soil fungi known to influence soil structure (van der Heijden et al., 2006). Finally, it is of high interest to conduct further research on the effects of reduced tillage techniques on different types of organic farming systems and their individual application in different environments (Cooper et al., 2016). In this context, the consideration of reduced tillage within strategies to increase yields in organic farming becomes of importance, as those strategies will most of all contribute to the general acceptance of organic principles in farming (Röös et al., 2018).

Useful further research will now be suggested.

Note the phrasing.

The significance of the further research is clarified.

References

Bargmann, C. (2018). Three ways to accelerate science. *Nature, 553*(7686), 19–21.

Brody, N. (1992). *Intelligence.* San Diego: Academic.

Bryant, G., & Aktipis, C. (2014). The animal nature of spontaneous human laughter. *Evolution and Human Behavior, 35*(4), 327–335.

Burgaleta, M. et al. (2012). Sex differences in brain volume are related to specific skills, not to general intelligence. *Intelligence, 40*(1), 60–68.

Caron, J. E. (2006). Silent slapstick film as ritualised clowning: the example of Charlie Chaplin. *Studies in American Humour, 3*(14), 5–22.

Chorley, A., & Bench-Capon, T. (2005). An empirical investigation of reasoning with legal cases through theory construction and application. *Artificial Intelligence and Law, 13*, 323–371.

Curry, O., & Dunbar, R. (2013). Sharing a joke: the effects of a similar sense of humor on affiliation and altruism. *Evolution and Human Behavior, 34*(2), 125–129.

Deary, I. J., Penke, L.,& Johnson, W. (2010). The neuroscience of human intelligence differences. *Nature Reviews Neuroscience, 11*, 201–211.

Dezecache, G., & Dunbar, R. (2012). Sharing the joke: the size of natural laughter groups. *Evolution and Human Behavior, 33*(6), 775–779.

Echavez, C. R., Mosawi, S., & Wilfreda R. E. Pilongo, L. (2016). *The other side of gender inequality: men and masculinities in Afghanistan.* Afghanistan Research and Evaluation Unit and Swedish Committee for Afghanistan. areu.org.af.

Eisend, M. (2018). Explaining the use and effects of humour in advertising: an evolutionary perspective. *International Journal of Advertising, 37*(4), 526–547.

Enloe, C. (2000 [1989]). *Bananas, beaches and bases.* Oakland: University of California Press.

Fine, C. (2010). *Delusions of gender: the real science behind sex differences.* London: Icon Books.

Gervais, M., & Wilson, D. (2005). The evolution and functions of laughter and humor: a synthetic approach. *The Quarterly Review of Biology, 80*(4), 395–430.

Goldstein, J. S. (2001). *War and gender: how gender shapes the war system and vice versa.* Cambridge: Cambridge University Press.

Gunsalus, C. K., McNutt, M. K., B. C., Martinson, Faulkner, L. R., & Nerem, R. M. (2019). Overdue: a US advisory board for research integrity. *Nature, 566*, 173–175.

Halpern, D. (2000). *Sex differences in cognitive abilities*. Mahwah: Lawrence Erlbaum.

Holt, M. K., Greif Green, J., Tsay-Vogel, M., Davidson, J., & Brown, C. (2016). Multidisciplinary approaches to research on bullying. *Adolescence Adolescent Research Review, 2*(1), 1–10.

Ikeda, D., & Phan, T. (2016). Toxic asset bubbles. *Economic Theory, 61*(2), 241–271.

Kay et al. (2019). Diversifcation, intensifcation and specialization: changing land use in Western Africa from 1800 BC to AD 1500. *Journal of World Prehistory, 32*(2), 179–228.

Kimura, D. (2002). Sex differences in the brain. *Scientific American, 12*(1s), 32–37.

Li, N., Griskevicius, V., Durante, K., Jonason, P., Pasisz, D., & Aumer, K. (2009). An evolutionary perspective on humor: sexual selection or interest indication? *Personality and Social Psychology Bulletin, 35*(7), 923–936.

Liu, J., & Lynn, R. (2015). Chinese sex differences in intelligence: some new evidence. *Personality and Individual Differences, 75*, 90–93.

McShane, B. B., & Gelman, A. (2017). Five ways to fix statistics: abandon statistical significance. *Nature, 551*(7681), 413–528.

Merga, M. K., & Roni, A. M. (2017). The influence of access to eReaders, computers and mobile phones on children's book reading frequency. *Computers and Education, 109*, 187–196.

Owren, M. J., & Bachorowski, J.-A. (2003). Reconsidering the evolution of nonlinguistic communication: the case of laughter. *Journal of Nonverbal Behavior, 27*(3), 183–200.

Penrose, L. S. (1963). *The biology of mental defect*. New York: Grune and Stratton.

Provine, R. (2017). Laughter as an approach to vocal evolution: the bipedal theory. *Psychonomic Bulletin & Review, 24*(1), 238–244.

Rajapaksa, D., Islam, M., & Managi, S. (2017). Natural capital depletion: the impact of natural disasters on inclusive growth. *Economics of Disasters and Climate Change, 1*(3), 233–244.

Ramachandran, V. (1998). The neurology and evolution of humor, laughter, and smiling: the false alarm theory. *Medical Hypotheses, 51*(4), 351–4.

Ross, M. D., Owren, M. J., & Zimmermann, E. (2009). Reconstructing the evolution of laughter in great apes and humans. *Current Biology, 19*(13), 1106–1111.

Seitz, S., Goebes, P., Puerta, V. L., Wittwer, R., Six, J., van der Heijedn, M. G. A., & Scholten, T. (2019). Conservation tillage and organic farming reduce soil erosion. *Agronomy for Sustainable Development, 39*(4). https://doi.org/10.1007/s13593-018-0545-z.

Shuster, S. (2012). The evolution of humor from male aggression. *Psychology Research and Behavior Management, 5*, 19–23.

Sorial, S. (2019). Anger, provocation and loss of self-control: what does 'losing it' really mean? *Criminal Law and Philosophy, 13*(2), 247–269.

van der Linden, D. Dunkel, C. S., & Madison, G. (2017). Sex differences in brain size and general intelligence. *Intelligence, 63*(C), 78–88.

Index

CPSIA information can be obtained
at www.ICGtesting.com
Printed in the USA
LVHW080543020221
678112LV00029B/328

9 781352 009163